The Static Caravan Story

The Static Caravan Story

BRITAIN'S FAVOURITE HOLIDAY HOME

ANDREW JENKINSON

The
History
Press

First published 2019

The History Press
The Mill, Brimscombe Port
Stroud, Gloucestershire, GL5 2QG
www.thehistorypress.co.uk

British Library Cataloguing in Publication Data.
A catalogue record for this book is available from the British Library.

ISBN 978 0 7509 8904 6

Typesetting and origination by The History Press
Printed in Turkey

Contents

Author Andrew Jenkinson stands alongside a 1962 Bluebird Senator at the Lakeland Manor Museum.

Foreword

From the early 1950s onwards, Britain's coastline would be invaded by caravans, or more accurately by the static or holiday caravan. These box-like designs would offer the British population a holiday by the sea, usually for a week or, if they were feeling flush, a fortnight! These sited permanent caravans offered the working classes all over the country a break from long hours spent working – mostly, back then, in factories.

The 1950s onwards witnessed a boom period, in which car ownership soared and the static caravan offered the masses their own 'cottages' by the sea or in the countryside. The humble caravan provided escapism and the chance for families to enjoy quality time together and forget their troubles. This book tells the story of how the static caravan evolved from a basic design and early construction to the luxury holiday home caravans of today. It also touches on the role of the static caravan as living accommodation after the Second World War, and on how some caravan sites became 'residential', designed for retired users, and how these statics then became fully-fledged retirement homes.

I hope the reader will be carried back to a time when life was simpler and the only way you contacted home was via a postcard!

Andrew Jenkinson

I have endeavoured to include as many brands, designs and ideas as possible in this book with most of the material taken from my own vast archives. I have also enlisted the help of *Park Home* and *Holiday Caravan Magazine* for missing parts of this story. All images are from the author's collection unless otherwise stated; in the event of any omission, please contact me care of the publishers.

1 The Static Caravan Story: How It All Began

We can look back to the gypsies for the idea of caravan living. They certainly inspired Dr Gordon Stables, a retired Naval officer who adapted the gypsy horse-drawn caravan for leisure in the early part of the twentieth century, and wrote of his adventures stopping in villages or by some wayside or seaside retreat. He named his caravan *Wanderer*, and it is now displayed at the Caravan & Motorhome Clubs Broadway touring site.

Dr Gordon Stables founded the idea of the Gentleman Gypsy with his horse-drawn 'flat on wheels', named *The Wanderer*, from the 1890s.

His books were read with interest by the gentry, who duly copied the idea, having a horse-drawn caravans built by a wagon builder and to share in Stables' adventures. Some of the wagon-built caravans were too heavy to be pulled by horses for any distance, and so instead these well-off 'gentleman gypsies' would transport their large wood-built and often ornate caravans via the railway, and leave them at various beauty spots for the summer, visiting them for holiday breaks. Subsequently these static caravans were brought back again for winter storage, or would remain in situ, looked after by a caretaker.

It wasn't until after the First World War that the car-pulled caravan came about – in 1919, pioneered by the Eccles Motor Transport Company. Producing mainly the first commercial car-towed caravans, as well as Showman Living Vans designed for show folk and gypsies. At around 5 metres in length these were designed like mobile flats. However, they were still being moved so were never left in one spot for any real length of time. The user of a car-pulled caravan would pitch up on land, after getting the landowner's permission. This would in many cases be the foundation stone for an official early caravan site in most cases. The formation of the Camping Club in 1901 and the then Caravan Club in 1907 had already paved the way for this.

The caravan user who toured would also at times find a spot that they particularly liked. In effect they would leave the caravan for a period of time, making the tourer now become static. No site had yet been developed for such a user, so many farmers would for extra income accept caravans on their land. Nobody took much notice of these caravans, even though they often accumulated rubbish and created an eyesore. Some of these static tourers would never move again, instead staying put as holiday accommodation.

By the '30s the car-pulled caravan had become more popular and affordable.

Above: These ornate and very heavy Gentleman Gypsy caravans were sent by train to a summer pitch, remaining 'static' for holidays.

Left: Some smaller caravans in the early 1900s were horse-drawn to a location and left there for summer breaks.

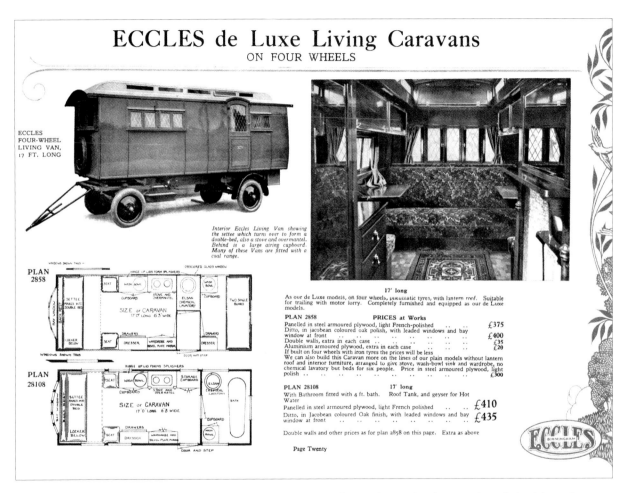

In the late 1920s, pioneer of the modern touring caravan/motorhome Eccles produced the idea of a luxury living caravan mainly for showmen.

It was no longer just a rich man's leisure activity; the middle classes were enjoying the holiday caravanning bug.

The '20s would see the rise of home-made caravans, which in most cases remained static due to poor towing performance. With a housing shortage and a surplus of ex-army vehicles after the First World War, those who were able converted some of the old mobile canteens into stop-gap living accommodation. Ex railway carriages were also used, with shack-type extensions added, and together they often formed shanty towns, which didn't prove popular with nearby homeowners. Though they were not used for holiday purposes, like the early static holiday homes they tended to become dilapidated, and eventually had to be cleared and scrapped.

Thus, with plots of land being used for permanent and holiday caravan living sites, the static holiday caravan was born.

The fashion was still for the holiday caravanner to be on the go and explore

A 1927 Eccles, designed to be towed to a plot then left for static use.

various parts of the country. However, some early manufacturers of caravans did design them for for semi-static use, such as Bertram Hutchings. His four-wheeler Concord model, at 6.39m in length, was considered too large for touring, so was usually pitched permanently to be used as a holiday base. By the 1930s the United States were forming trailer parks, designed for holiday static caravans and and permanent home trailers. They had mains-connected water and power, and proper road access.

After the First World War houses were in short supply and many used old horse-drawn caravans as permanent homes.

Anything with wheels was used to live in. Conditions were poor with no sanitation or facilities.

The early 1930s in the US saw the rise of what could be described as the first mobile home. Known as the 'demountable', this one-bedroomed bungalow design was manufactured in two separate halves, in the same way as today's park homes. It was completely prefabricated with all work being carried out at the factory; the idea was then to deliver it to a site on two trucks, one for each half. Once at the site, the two halves were unloaded then levelled and assembled. The idea was ahead of its time. During the Second World War the US government bought 46,000 trailers to house war workers, with trailer parks designed like small towns: chalet-style trailers with two bedrooms for couples and larger units for families were provided, all well serviced with amenities.

Back in the UK, the idea of a specially built holiday static caravan was still not on the horizon. In the 1930s there was an increasing number of tourer manufacturers. They built caravans up to 5m in length for touring or using in one spot, say for a summer season, before moving it again in winter to store when not in use. Construction followed coachbuilding techniques, with timber framework and panelling on each side. Insulation wasn't seen as necessary, and most caravans had a paraffin stove or solid fuel for heating.

The larger horse-drawn units that had been used before the rise of the car-pulled caravan were very heavy and not easy to move around. Thus they were now left to rot, or in some cases purchased as a place to live, during the interwar period. Others were bought for use as holiday cottages. One such user was BBC big band leader Reginald King, a popular broadcaster and recording artist of the early '30s. King and his wife had purchased one of these old-style four-wheel horse-drawn caravans and laid it to rest in the corner of a field in the South Downs. The Kings and their dog Whisky used the static caravans for weekends. It had a bedroom, dining room and kitchen. The Kings had a small outdoor area around the sited caravan with a large

garden bench seat providing views of the Downs. Were the Kings pioneers – the first celebrity caravan holiday-home owners? Certainly the pair kept the location of the caravan a closely guarded secret from the media, to ensure they were left alone! They had a ten-minute walk from the sea and claimed the caravan was more like a bungalow in size, yet without the outlay. But the Kings didn't set a trend in this market as yet. It was a change in the law that would spark some interest in static holiday caravans.

The USA had taken the lead with mass production of static caravan units, but the UK market was, at this time, nonexistent. A couple of UK manufacturers heard about the US idea, and a couple of types did start to be made, but these designs were to be quite simple; and as yet they were little used, as there were no official sites for them.

However, as previously mentioned, many old caravans, army vehicles and train carriages were forming unofficial sites; and this was increasingly becoming a problem.

The BBC 1930s band leader Reginald King's old horse-drawn caravan was permanently sited at a secret location on the South Downs.

The public wanted these so-called 'caravanners' – perhaps wrongly classified in this case – banned. Instead, a 1936 Act would tidy up the sites that were springing up – mainly on the coast, North Wales being especially popular – and force some planning. The Act controlled movable dwellings and was aimed at preventing overcrowding of touring static caravans. Site owners now needed to apply for licences allowing land to be used for camping/caravanning for no more than forty-two or 102 consecutive days, depending on the licence. A further licence had to be granted by the local authority to either the landowner or the caravanner. A licence wasn't required, though, if a caravan owner owned the land it was sited on and it was used by family. Better control would at least take the sting out of the bad name caravanners received. With some planning and legislation sites became a little more organised, which would finally allow the UK static caravan market to begin to grow.

FUN FACT

Rich caravan users of the 1920s and '30s might also take a servant on their break to do any chores; they would have to sleep in a tent.

Raven Caravans in Thames Ditton Surrey had been an early caravan manufacturer for car-pulled caravans as well as early motorhomes. As Eccles had, it would build to customer requirements from its standard ranges. From 1930 Eccles built 15ft caravans as 'holiday cottages' – this marketing was a romantic ideal typical of the period. In 1936/37 Raven also received a request from a customer to build a caravan cottage. But unlike a normal touring caravan, it was only to be towed to its destination and then pitched up. So the designer and owner

Caravan sites sprang up by coasts in the early 1930s. They often used old horse-drawn types and even converted railway carriages.

of Raven, Mr Wilkinson Cox, designed a rectangular body shell on a four-wheel chassis – two small wheels at the front on a spindle or drawbar for easy pitching and two small wheels under the main body at the rear. It was possibly only ever to be towed once or twice in its lifetime. It had two interior compartments, each with separate entrances: a small kitchen and large living room that converted to a bedroom to sleep two at night. With no requirement to be suitable for towing, the constraints were loosened, and loose furniture could be used in the Cottage: wicker freestanding chairs and table in the living room, which was spacious, and settees that became single beds. Its windows were quite large for that period and there was a fireplace in the living room, complete with mantelpiece. Hot water was provided and the kitchen came fitted with a gas cooker; gas was only just being used in caravans at that time, and the Raven Cottage also boasted gas lighting too. The Cottage was built using

FUN FACT

Early caravan owners had to purchase a spade for disposing of lavatory waste.

triple panelling, thus it could be used all year round, allowing people to live in. The interior walls were polished oak and the kitchen was open plan into the dining room, so it was ahead of its time in many ways. Raven reported that the Country Cottage had caused interest with several more ordered.

Strangely Eccles, by now the biggest caravan manufacturer of this period, didn't go down this route, possibly because the Raven was quite simple in many ways and Eccles was better known as a manufacturer of quality tourers and more ornate showman's living vans by this time. No sales records on the Cottage

have the only factory in the world specially built and equipped for the production of Motor Caravans

FOR USE AS A HOLIDAY COTTAGE

THE CARAVANS ILLUSTRATED ON THIS PAGE ARE BUILT ON SPECIAL DE-LUXE LINES, THEY ARE VERY ROOMY AND COMPLETELY FURNISHED, THEY ARE BUILT TO ANSWER THE PURPOSE OF A MOVABLE WEEK-END COTTAGE OR SEASIDE BUNGALOW, THEY CAN BE TOWED FROM PLACE TO PLACE BY A 20 H.P. CAR OR LARGER. THE PLANS SET OUT ARE GIVEN WITH A VIEW TO SHOWING HOW LAYOUTS MAY BE ARRANGED, WE, HOWEVER, ARE OUT TO MEET THE REQUIREMENTS OF OUR CUSTOMERS, AND SHOULD BE HAPPY TO MODIFY THE PLANS OR DRAW OUT NEW SO THAT YOUR WISHES IN EVERY DETAIL MAY BE CONSIDERED.

PLAN 2848. 15 ft. long, 6 ft. 2ins. wide. Two compartment Caravan, to sleep four people (two in each compartment) built with Ventilated Lantern Roof, Double Panelled, Leaded Casement Windows, extra large Bay Window at front (and back if desired). To this plan and furniture, or may be supplied to sleep two, and the back compartment made into a Bathroom, with Bath, "Elsan" Chemical Lavatory and Washbowl.

PLAN 28108. 17 ft. long, 6 ft. 5in. wide. Two compartment Caravan, to sleep two people, with Bathroom in rear compartment. May also be supplied to sleep four, but the back compartment is made into a Bedroom instead of a Bathroom. It may also be built with Vestibule Entrance, and Chemical Lavatory, opposite the door, in separate compartment. Double Panelled, Ventilated Lantern Roof, Leaded Casement Windows, extra large Bay Window at front (and back if desired). Built on four wheels The description of the separate units of furniture would be the same as the 11 ft. on page 20.

Eccles 15 ft. Caravan on two wheels. Note canvas strip along side above door, shows where Lean-to Tent is attached.

Eccles 17 ft. Caravan on four wheels. 15 ft. Caravans are frequently built like this.

PRICES. Light or Dark Polish, painted to choice of colour. Built on two wheels. **£350.** Built on four wheels. **£380.** If built with Bathroom, prices on application according to tanks required, hot and cold water, etc.

PRICES. Light or Dark Polish, painted to choice of colour. To sleep four, without Bathroom. **£420.** To sleep two, with Bathroom, prices on application according to tanks required, hot and cold water.

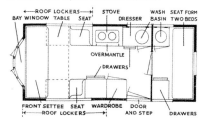

Caravans of this size are nearly always built to special order, and the photographs and plans on this page are submitted to give an idea of what can be done. If you are interested in any large Caravan we shall be happy to learn your requirements, and can then submit to you particulars of what we have built, or prepare estimate and designs for your approval. Our experience is considerable and is entirely at your disposal.

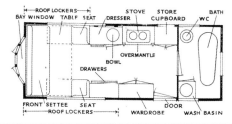

By the 1930s Eccles developed the 'holiday cottage', which purchasers could order with variations of layout from a standard design.

Raven, another early caravan/motorhome producer, saw a potential of the static holiday caravan, naming its take the Cottage.

The interior of the Cottage reflected its name, with gas lights and solid fuel stove. It was seen as fine for year-round living.

exist, but its popularity showed that non-caravanners liked the idea of a caravan, but one which had more space and home comforts than a tourer. This idea was to be picked up by established caravan dealers Wellford's of Warninglid. Wellford's took it a step further, by marketing the service of delivery and setting up the unit on a plot for the owner.

Balmforth Sanderson, a Yorkshire caravan manufacturer, designed and built a prefabricated static caravan, 5.48m length by 2.22m, to be sold by Wellford's. Named the Cara-bung, it was based on the bungalow concept. With no towing gear nor chassis with suspension, construction costs could be kept low. Its £145 price tag included a twin burner stove, paraffin lights and oil-fired radiator. It could sleep four and had two rooms and a kitchen, two lavatories and wardrobes. It was well-built, but was intended not as a luxury tourer but a holiday weekend retreat. The Cara-bung was sold as a caravan that would be sent to a site where

Balmforth's Cara-bung was sold through dealers Wellford's, which would arrange transport and pitching up for static holiday use.

the owners could use it during every summer. Yet marketing it would prove hard. Although the press clearly saw the potential for caravan parks in rural and coastal beauty spots for holidaymakers wanting a 'cottage' without the price tag, conservative thinking and the threat of another war looming would stall the idea from taking hold with the public. Balmforth's idea didn't catch on yet.

FUN FACT

Toilets in early caravans were frowned upon by some due to their noises being easily heard when in use!

Some also recognised the potential for caravan sites to be used for year-round living. Some predicted that owners of houses would sell up and live in Cara-bung style static caravans, with the cash this released being used as a pension. Balmforth Sanderson also produced a living version of the Cara-bung, named the Balmforth Parkholme - a name that was adopted and adapted by park homes and endures to this day. At 5.48m in length and 2.22m in width, the Parkholme offered accommodation for up to four and was equipped with gas and a solid fuel stove. It was truly ahead of its time.

BALMFORTH "PARKHOLME"

DESIGNED AND EQUIPPED FOR PERMANENT OCCUPATION

4 BERTH. 18 ft. 6ins. long x 7 ft. 3 ins. wide

NEW SPECIFICATION

BODY Good quality timber frames. Hardboard exterior panels. Walls and ceiling lined with insulation board. One door. Steps to door. Windows at sides and ends, seven windows open.

UNDERGEAR Axle and springs of ample capacity. Easy clean wheels, 7·00 x 16 tyres. Brace-operated adjustable legs. Steel tow bar with automatic brake.

FITTINGS

Two wardrobes (one with folding doors; to divide caravan at night. Small washbowl cabinet in bedroom. Two bed settees with deep spring mattress cushions. Lockers under. Double top table with two drawers. Kitchen partition with serving hatch.

Kitchen cabinet with drawer and ventilated food cupboard. Sink with waste.

Cooking stove recess with cupboard for gas cylinder. Gas lighting and cooking. Coal Stove with oven. Wired for mains electric. Lino. Sunk mat-well to door. One mirror. Outside painted cream and green. Inside cream walls and ceiling. Pale green fittings.

WHY WAIT FOR HOUSES ?

BUILT BY
BALMFORTH & CO.
EAST HESLERTON
Near MALTON . YORKS
Telephone : SHERBURN 57   Established 1908

Balmforth gave their 1930s holiday/living caravan the name of 'Parkholme' – reminiscent of today's 'park homes'. Had they invented it unknowingly?

The seeds had been sown, and following the 1936 Public Health Act static sites for bungalow-style caravans became more of a possibility.

First though, came war, and with it rationing, blackouts and the blitz – all of which would leave their mark on the caravanning community. Those who kept their touring caravans during the war had no petrol due to rationing. Many caravans were laid up on farm fields, some never to be moved again. Into the '60s and '70s it was a common sight to see old caravans parked up in a fields, left to rot.

FUN FACT

A caravanner claimed he saw caravans bounce off the ground when a bomb exploded nearby during an air raid.

On the other hand, caravans helped the war effort by providing temporary housing with some manufacturers turning out basic models to this end. With so much of Britain's production capacity dedicated to the war effort, the demand for caravans would outstrip supply, leading to over inflated prices and poor quality in design and construction. They often had a poor chassis, due to steel shortages and were primitive in design and overall construction. Insulation was virtually nonexistent and in the early part of the Second World War severe winters meant they were ice boxes. Meanwhile. If they were equipped with a gas fire, the obligatory blackout sheets on the windows meant no air could pass through for ventilation, resulting in some caravan dwellers dying of carbon monoxide poisoning!

Charles Ensor's 1943 design (the Ensor Wellington) was truly ahead of its time, being a square chalet-style home instead of a typical rectangular towing-style design. It had a lounge, bedroom, kitchen and toilet room. Few were built, but the idea of a living unit closer to a house than a vehicle marked an important step in static caravan home development. Some dealers would sell literally anything that resembled a caravan to those desperate for any kind of home, and the trade would soon get a bad press.

The necessities of wartime had, however, proved that caravans *could* be lived in, and after the conflict ended manufacturers would provide new living designs, though still mainly in the 5–6m length. What was until then described as a holiday/living van was the size of most touring caravans in 2019. Some of the caravan manufacturers who had turned their production to war efforts would fail to return once peace arrived. Others, including Eccles, learned much about new ideas of construction and mass production and would grow bigger after the war.

2 The 1950s and 1960s

The National Caravan Council (NCC) was founded by Bill Whiteman, an early pioneer of the caravanning press, in May 1939, with the Caravan Club, the Camping and Caravanning Club and the Royal Automobile Club (RAC) all joining. The body was to fight the corner for manufacturers but also would play a major role in developing and managing caravan sites as they entered a boom period after the Second World War. As austerity gradually gave way to a new, more carefree Britain, the romantic ideal of the holiday home became appealing. For many families having a caravan holiday meant fresh air, adventure and a chance to finally forget the horrors of wartime. The UK's coastline would begin to see a change as sites appeared even up to cliff edges, while caravan manufacturers increasingly designed statics to be more home-like and mirroring contemporary design trends. The static would also become a mobile home for those returning from the armed forces or who struggled to find accommodation in the housing shortage of the late 1940s and early 1950s while Britain recovered from wartime austerity.

As shortages eased and war work dried up, pre-war manufacturers such as Eccles got back to work. The NCC played an important role in pushing the development of the caravan forward in this period. It contacted suppliers to gather materials for caravan manufacturers to inspect. New materials would see advances made in construction techniques. Aluminium framework was tried by some makers, and new insulation materials, such as fibreglass matting, were introduced. Formica, laminated plastics, alloy window frames, new sealants and aluminium replaced hardboard exterior panels. Clear Perspex was ideal for roof vents and new glues proved superior to pre-war ones. Mass-production techniques, perfected during the war, were also beginning to be employed by manufacturers of caravans,

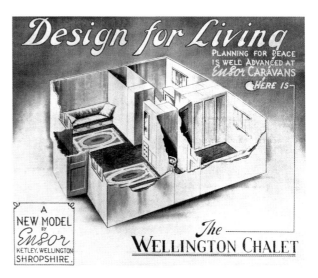

In 1943 Ensor Caravans was thinking ahead to after the war with this Chalet design, named the Wellington Chalet.

with new technology such as jig sections revolutionising the industry.

Eccles's first mass-produced caravan, the Enterprise, was launched for 1946. Only 4.26m in length, it slept four and was classed as a 'holiday van', ideal for sitting. In fact Eccles would supply over forty Enterprises for US army personnel as accommodation. Paladin caravans, a

The Eccles Enterprise was a 4.44m-long holiday caravan from 1946, Eccles learnt a lot about mass-production techniques during the war.

In 1942 these Ensor touring caravans were laid-up and remained 'static'. Many caravans like these would not be moved and were used as permanent holiday caravans.

The
JENKINSON
Mobile Cottage

If you want a van to live in, as distinct from holiday touring then surely your first requirement is as much **SPACE** as possible.

But space costs money and even to-day, when prices are lower, the large van still costs from £800 up to over £2,000. Yet here is a van 19ft. 1in. by 7ft. 5in. with 6ft. 8in. headroom at only £650. It has an end kitchen with full-size gas cooker, separate bedroom and loads of cupboards. Moreover, it is well made with first-class aluminium walls and roof.

And you can plan the Mobile Cottage if you wish, to your own special requirements at no extra expense unless you want many extra fittings in it

Indeed, for a wait of about three weeks, you can have a larger version 22ft. by 7ft. 6in. with a bathroom for under £1,000.

And the Mobile Cottage isn't made by just anyone. It is made for A. S. Jenkinson by the famous Paladin folk on a good Southall or other proprietary chassis, with a Brockhouse hitch. It has Easyclean wheels, brace operated jacks, room for a Pither stove, glass fronted cupboards, lavatory if desired, and other refinements. Surely, if you want a HOME and your pocket isn't deep, this is the van for you at : **£650 !**

A. S. JENKINSON
BATH ROAD, TAPLOW, BUCKS. *Telephone:* Maidenhead 2610

Jenkinson's, a dealer based in Taplow, commissioned Paladin Trailers in 1947 to build the Mobile Cottage for static holiday/live-in use.

small 1939 pre-war maker run by George Holder, also saw a boom in caravans in the late 1940s and began making coach-style caravans called Trailer vans. With strong construction they were meant for living in rather than for the holiday market. A.S. Jenkinson (no relation to the author) had set up a business selling caravans in the mid 1940s and by 1946 had several makes on his Taplow forecourt. Jenkinson was impressed with the pre-war bungalow-type design from Balmforth and had Paladin build a 5.78m long by 2.28m

wide Mobile Cottage priced at £600, with a larger model, 6.7m in length, also available. Penarth Caravans in Wales, a new company, also built a very similar design, hoping to capture this new market for the 1950s. Interestingly, Balmforth also continued to make the pre-war Cara-bung, but by 1947 had launched a larger more luxury version named the Princess, for sale at a price of £850. The Princess was designed as a living van with all services, including a bath. In 1949, the International Caravan Company, based in

BALMFORTH & CO
EAST-HESLERTON
MALTON, YORKS

22 FEET LONG

Contains :
  LARGE LOUNGE
  (2 Bedrooms at night)
  also Child's Bedroom
  KITCHEN
  BATHROOM
    with Toilet

THE BALMFORTH " EMPRESS " £875

Tel.:
Sherborn 57

7' 6" WIDE 7' HIGH

Anthracite Heating Stove
Gas and Mains Electric for
                    Lighting
Gas Cooker
Water, equipment includes
Base Tank, Roof Cistern
Water Heater
Taps to Sinks and Bath

In the late 1940s Balmforth returned to the idea of the Cara-bung with the more luxury Empress, which cost £849.

Liverpool, produced its Homobile, also designed for living in. It had four rooms and came with all mains facilities, but its success was limited.

With holidaying Brits heading for boarding houses for their summer holidays, trying to get 'digs' was nigh on impossible at peak times and some of those who ran the boarding houses treated their guests more like prisoners! The caravan was the obvious answer, and owners who had sited tourers began to sublet to neighbours and friends. Site owners didn't mind too much, since the visitors kept a small site shop or milk delivery busy through the summer. The caravan holiday then was seen as an ideal way to get away from the daily grind of working life and still bombed damaged areas.

The 1949 Homobile was designed for living or as holiday use.

After the war many couples hired a caravan for a week's holiday, escaping the constraints of boarding house rules!

This early 1950s image shows the true spirit of the static caravan holiday with many families making new friends and enjoying themselves.

After the war new caravan concerns sprang up. One was Berkeley, which produced the Baronet in 1948, a holiday caravan with many innovations.

With this demand for caravans, a new generation of manufacturers sprang up. Charles Panter with his brother Frank (who later went onto retail caravans) had a company that had produced furniture and repaired planes in wartime. After the war this work had dropped off, and he began searching for new ideas to put his machinery and staff to use. Observing that the caravan market was booming, he turned his Bedfordshire factory to producing caravans. The new company took the name Berkeley Coachworks. Its first model was the Carapartment – later renamed the Baronet – launched in late 1947.

Designed using ideas learnt in the war, the Baronet was quite advanced with a front-end kitchen, water tanks for showering, mains electrics and Perspex frameless windows, and clip-off wheel spats as used on aircraft (showing the direct inspiration Panter took from his wartime work). It was constructed using Onazote, a type of rubber, sandwiching the interior and exterior panels. A one-piece aluminium roof replaced the lead-painted canvas used pre-war. The 4.26m Baronet was designed as a tourer or holiday caravan. Sold at a price over £1,000, it was too costly to succeed, and Panter's US tour to sell it in the States was a failure.

Berkeley would next aim at a more conventional design, with models such as the Ambassador, which became one of its most successful. At 6.7m in length, it offered the holiday caravanner and those wanting a living van a spacious interior, two bedrooms, a washroom and a kitchen that also came with matching upholstered seats that slid under the kitchen unit when not in use. By the mid 1950s the company was producing a suite of popular caravan designs. These included the Governor, which had fold-down rear-end extension panels, and the 1955 Domicile, whose large windows and sleeping accommodation for up to six made it an ideal holiday site caravan. It had a front porch and a side pull-out extension that added 4.2m of extra width, but which folded away to allow it be towed to a new site by a large car. And Panter's imagination really ran wild when he produced the double-decker 1952 Statesman – a house on wheels. The Statesman was designed for young couples wanting a home that could be moved if job circumstances changed; ingenious-sounding, but it didn't sell well. When a fire at the Berkeley factory (a big risk at caravan factories) destroyed around ten Statesmans, his dealers remarked that it just meant they had fewer of them to try to sell!

Left: The Berkeley Governor showed off the ingenious creativity of Panter, with its end being extendable once it was sited.

All your comforts doubly extended...

Berkeley Governor General Mk. II

The rear extension which has made the Berkeley Governor so popular a residential caravan has been adapted to both ends of the Governor-General. For towing the overall length is 25 ft. including tow bar, but on the site this is increased to a spacious 34 ft. with fine kitchen and bathroom, one permanent bedroom and a big lounge and dinette convertible into two more double bedrooms. The extensions are simple to operate, absolutely rigid and weatherproof.

The Governor-General is the biggest model in the Berkeley range of specialised caravans—made possible at popular prices through Berkeley's unique production resources and long-term planning. Read the specification overleaf for a more detailed picture of this wonderful home-on-wheels.

Berkeley "AMBASSADOR"
A home to delight you . . . and take where you will

 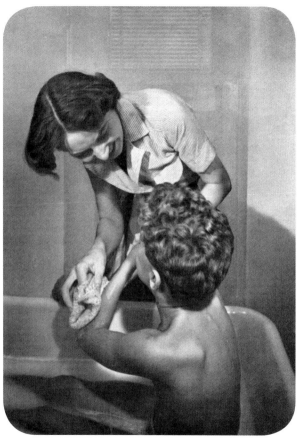

Above: The interior of the Ambassador. It had upholstered stools in the kitchen and even a bath.

Left: By 1950 the Ambassador, a 6.7m-long design, boasted an end kitchen and was seen as a perfect holiday or living van.

The 1952 Statesman, Panter's double-decker live-in caravan proved a flop, despite all the PR.

Memories

Rose Hinchliffe remembered living in a Governor:

Having just got married, this caravan was the answer to our housing problem. The ends folding down gave us much more room and we had our first child a year or so after. We sold it after finding a house, but we loved that Berkeley though it could be drafty!

Frank Panter went into retail, while Charles's production rates would continue to increase, putting the town of Biggleswade on the map. However, some of the models he produced did flop and badly, including his folder designs – mainly down to problems with durability and poor headroom. He had, though, sparked imaginations, as other manufacturers, such as Marston, Terra Coach, and Country Life, also produced two-storey designs in the same period. The Montrose dealership in Cheshire

The Terracoach double-decker also found few buyers. Like the Statesman, its hardboard sides meant durability was not good.

Luxurious Living...

The Peak Diplomat M K II

Above: Built for large Cheshire dealers Montrose, the Peak Diplomat was a full two-storey caravan. Sales were limited but those sold were used as living vans.

Left: Interior of the Diplomat emulated a cottage styled interior, note the stairs to the right.

commissioned Peak Caravans in Derby to produce a luxury two-storey 7m-long living van with solid-fuel heating that combined a cottage feel with the modern trends of the '50s. But sales were stark and the Diplomat was dropped too.

High-end manufacturer Coventry Steel, a pre-war caravan maker owned by innovator Clifford Dawtrey, introduced the Phantom Knight after the war. It too was ahead of its time, with a Perspex-finished kitchen and bathroom, a central heating system, and lighting designed by Dawtrey as well. Costing over £1,000, it was expensive. Dawtrey decided to try and design distinctive living vans, but cost was a problem due to his fanciful ideas, such as a garden roof and beds that would drop from the ceiling. He was brilliantly inventive, but business sense was not his forte. On his death in 1958 the industry truly lost an innovator.

Other new makers joining the boom included Bailey, Bluebird, Pemberton, Willerby, Marston, Stanmore, Donnington

The Coventry Steel Phantom 47 was expensive but came with higher specifications than most middle-class houses of the time.

Nene Valley, Normandie, Alperson (Sprite) Summerdale, Colonial, Bessacarr, Cresta, Beverley, Campmaster, Overlander, Carahomes, Columbia, Comet, Country Life, Coronet, Riley's/Lynton, Dovedale, Fairholme, Fairview, Lissett, Lister, Premier, Shannon, Speak, Sipson, Sun Regent, Astral and Travelmaster – and they were joined by plenty of smaller concerns too. Most of these likewise made tourers, but would increasingly concentrate on static holiday caravans and living vans.

'Caravan' was still very much the term used, whether it referred to a static caravan or a tourer. This terminology was to blight the industry, due to the stigma associated with poor caravan sites – especially those that had appeared after the war as demobbed military personnel followed work opportunities and needed a home. Despite the 1936 Public Health Act, poor maintenance of sites and the accumulation of rubbish remained problematic as caravans were illegally parked on demolition sites or wasteland.

The NCC would fight to enforce new national standards both for sites and manufacturers of caravans. Standards for construction were set and caravan manufacturers were encouraged to keep to such rules for overall general safety in design, particularly those concerning ventilation. A caravan with the NCC badge came to give the buyer confidence that it was a professional construction.

By the early 1950s, caravan buyers demanded more space, giving rise to a new market for larger living units. Willerby Caravans, a new manufacturer from 1946, spotted this demand and quickly began making larger models that provided great value for the price tag. In doing so the company transformed the East Yorkshire area of Hull and its surrounding villages and towns into the caravan-manufacturing capital of the UK; it remains so in 2019. The 1951 Willerby Home, which retailed at £450, provided 6.7m-long fully furnished accommodation for up to four, using either as a holiday or living caravan. For a further

Above: After the war sights like this were not uncommon; the top is actually part of a plane's fuselage.

Right: Old buses were being lived in on spare land; former horse-drawn caravans became homes too.

£195 a deluxe version was available. It was soon in steady demand.

The Willerby Home went on to be sold as a twin unit adjoined in the middle with a corridor, providing more space. This method of increasing the space available was popular. It was used by Paladin in its 4.5m-long Wisdom, which could be doubled in size by adding a second section connected by a veranda. The duplex extension consisted of a bedroom and bathroom, while the other section was the basic Wisdom tourer. It didn't sell well.

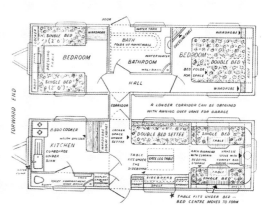

Above: Willerby twinned its Home models via a corridor; one side was for day living, the other for a bedroom and bathroom.

The 1951 Range of WILLERBY MASTERPIECES

THE PERFECT 'WILLERBY HOME'

22 ft. LONG
7 ft. 6 in. WIDE
6 ft. 9 in. HEADROOM

£450
EX WORKS
FULLY FURNISHED

Supreme in a class of its own!

THE WILLERBY HOME DE-LUXE	£595 0 0
THE AMAZING WILLERBY DE-LUXE 15'6" × 6'6" × 6'3"	£299 10 0
THE WILLERBY JUNIOR MARK I, 12'3" × 6'3" × 6'6" (3-berth)	£205 0 0
THE WILLERBY JUNIOR MARK II (4 berth)	£215 0 0

Right: Willerby's Home of 1951 proved a good seller with its design and finishes, and established Hull as a caravan manufacturing centre.

Paladin followed Willerby's idea. Its 4.26m Wisdom tourer using an extension with veranda and a duplicate Wisdom shell with a different interior fit out.

Pemberton, a manufacturor that was to become a major force due to its honest, practical layouts, was started in 1946 by brothers Eric and Norman Rigby and by the early 1950s they were manufacturing such models as the Dusk, a 5m-long holiday caravan that slept four. Pembertons, with their distinctive design, were to become big sellers to site owners for hiring out a few years later. The company would go on to buy out rivals Cresta of Hull and Dovedale of Blackpool, and also have its own plastics manufacturing division and chassis maker.

Meanwhile Bill Knott of Poole was overseeing the expansion of his own caravan empire. Knott and his father had been producing very low-cost caravans before the war under the Midland brand, but from 1946 the Ringwood Road factory took the trading name Bluebird. Like Pemberton, during the 1950s Bluebird's growth was phenomenal, despite criticism that its vans were 'rough around the edges'. They were cheap and provided

THE SIXTEEN FEET BY SEVEN FEET

Pemberton

" Dusk "

★*Planned and Built for*

your comfort.

Pemberton would become a big name in static holiday caravans; early models such as the Dusk would establish the marque.

THE   "BLUEBIRD"

DEFIANT
FOLD-AWAY   "HOME"

FULLY   INSULATED   **£315**   EX   WORKS

Knott's Bluebird caravans were cheap and found favour among early static caravan buyers, though quality wasn't at its best in the early days.

ordinary folk with the chance to own their own holiday getaway. His factory was running twenty-four hours a day, and with improved production techniques Bluebird could turn out over 100 units a week. New models included the Magnet, Forget-me-Knot, Conquest and Heritage. Bluebird soon became the leader in the industry, garnering large export orders and allowing Knott to buy out Premier Homes and Sun-Regent Caravans, plus Bournemouth golf course and a caravan site which he added 350 Bluebird holiday homes that would be hired out. Bluebird also expanded into horse boxes and coach-built motorhomes by 1958. Neither Bluebird nor Pemberton joined the NCC; neither liked the idea of being told how to make their caravans!

Memories

Roger Partridge:

My grandparents wanted a holiday caravan, so Granddad put his skills into action and built a 5m caravan and had it towed to a site in Hampshire. It had a front-end kitchen and dining room plus a chemical loo and lounge area, and slept four. In the mid '50s we had great holidays there, as a child playing with all the other kids. I have fond memories of caravan holidays!

Roger Partridge's grandfather sits outside his home built static caravan in Hampshire. (Courtesy of Roger Partridge)

With demand at such a high, all the major manufacturers – including Berkeley, Paladin and Eccles – were experiencing similar booms and the number of factories was on the increase.

One difficulty with the new larger caravans was that they were problematic to transport. Heavy-duty road wheels were fitted and they were towed to site, but the process was slow, and many of these large caravans proved unstable at speeds above 25mph! As a result, lorries began to be used to transport larger statics. Nonetheless, many were fitted with road wheels, even though they couldn't realistically be used; manufacturers didn't begin to fit the small transport wheels until the mid 1960s. In 1952, Vernon Industries' Deeside van was designed to be easily towed by a car, with winding handles used to make it wider once it reached the site. Ingenious though it might have sounded as an idea, the Deeside flopped – possibly due to its eye-watering £1,795 price tag.

Specialist caravan transporters delivered holiday caravans/mobile homes. This is a Nene Valley Waveney from 1965.

And of course, as the caravans grew, site owners were finding that pitches had to be made larger too. But this more often than not saw lines of caravans appearing on the coastline of the UK. Sites were mostly poorly laid-out and loo blocks were not the norm, with owners having to use a chemical loo that was then disposed of in a pit! Caravans were also poorly sited too, but strangely nobody really questioned such makeshift arrangements. Local councils though would soon begin to clamp down, applying rules on the number of caravans and how the site had to be planned out.

Sites sprang up in the early '50s, often unplanned, and vans were sited where they were left.

The late '50s Holgates family site in Silverdale was developed and heavily invested over the years. Many good sites began like this. (Courtesy of Holgates)

In Lancashire the Holgate caravan company was making mainly touring caravans at its works in Accrington, formed just after the Second World War. Founder Billy Holgate with his wife Miriam realised in the early '50s that the caravanning boom was sure to see more demand for sites – and good ones too. In 1956, at Middlebarrow plane near Silverdale, close to the shoreline, the couple found a spot to begin a small site. From scrubland previously populated with old railway carriages and the odd old caravan, the couple with their teenage sons set about making a proper site with roads, planned pitches and a reception hut. In 1956 Holgate Caravan Parks Ltd was formed, and through the late 1950s, profits were into new pitches.

Holgate stopped manufacturing caravans in 1964 to concentrate on the caravan park instead. Toilet blocks, proper roadways and a shop saw the site grow. From the late '60s, guests were expecting more and more facilities on site; they wanted more than just a static stuck in a field. The Holgate park expanded through the 1970s and '80s, with the addition of a swimming pool, and further facilities – a café, bar, games room and even crazy golf.

By the early 1990s Billy's son Frank was running the site with his son Michael and daughter Susan and Frank's wife Judith. New sites were acquired and new facilities added as profits were consistently reinvested to improve facilities and increase visitor numbers.

Site owners could fill all their land with caravans – often a mix of holiday and living vans – making sites in many cases crowded. In winter the holiday units were often moved off their pitches, to stop owners using them during the out-of-season period. Caravans would get damaged when they were moved, but van owners could never prove this, of course. I remember visiting, as a child in the late '60s, a site in the Lake District in winter where all the static holiday caravans had been pushed into one corner of the site!

Memories

Roger Partridge on sites:

The site was grassed (ankle deep after cutting!) with a rough road on its perimeter, and there was a small hut-type shop where basics could be purchased. Even though the site had expanded no loo blocks were built. These wouldn't appear till later in the '50s. Because of the slope of the ground the rear of the caravan was around a metre off the ground with a pile of bricks supporting it – not very professional!

The caravan press, who would also help shape the caravan site and the holiday caravan, reported in various magazines on the latest new maker, site opening and latest models. And with new manufacturers constantly springing up, some to last months only, keeping a check on the market wasn't easy.

Eccles and Balmforth were struggling in the static van market sector and instead decided to focus on touring caravans. Eccles did do some larger models that were designed for travellers and showmen, and also models such as the Imperial, Eversure and Enchantress that were classed as large tourers but were usually sited for holiday use or for living in. With hardboard being replaced by aluminium for exterior panels and new anodised window frames, as well as dedicated chassis and upholstery manufacturers (though Willerby/Pemberton did have

Out-of-season holiday caravans were taken off the site and stored. This is Bispham Lodge caravan site around 1949.

Memories

Glynn Waterfall:

Living in Manchester in the mid '50s meant a caravan holiday near the sea was so exciting and a real treat. My parents bought a Willerby from the early '50s and had it sited at the Bispham caravan site near Blackpool, it had a café with simple fare and the site was very basic but I had so much fun and dad always wore a tie!

Glyn Waterfall's parents' Willerby caravan around the early 1950s. (Courtesy of Glyn Waterfall)

their own factories for chassis and soft furnishings manufacture), the industry was getting better organised.

Dealers too were better placed to supply repairs, parts and accessories as the market grew. Some dealers would buy sites and then sell to customers a caravan already in place. Greenwoods (MG Caravan dealers) would tow 6.7m-long Pembertons to Scotland and pitch up on rented land to hire out the static caravans.

Sites continued to be improved, for living vans especially, though some were still like slums, with poor roads and facilities such as mains water still not available. In summer months, when the weather was

Dealers such as MG Caravans at Todmorden sold statics and tourers, as well as providing sites and a parts-plus-delivery service. (Courtesy of Martin Greenwood)

Pathfinder Village near Exeter had been owned and run as a touring site by the Horton brothers from the early 1930s. By the late 1940s they had thirty pitches in 40 acres, which all had mains and road ways to them. The Horton brothers anticipated the growth of the static caravan home and began to add these vans to their site. The Hortons also added a shop,

Static caravan owners had few facilities on most sites, but it didn't stop families enjoying the freedom of such holidays and weekends. Note the dustbin and washing drying!

good, sites were a hive of activity, with children playing and even the parents joining in for games of football and cricket. With no TV and just a radio and a pack of cards for entertainment, many static owners would socialise and many friends for life were made through the caravan holiday. Even on sites with living vans, folk were friendly and helped each other.

Parks' better planning and neat plots saw newly-weds and retired folk buy into the mobile home lifestyle.

then a café, a church, a bank, a doctor's surgery and even a hairdressers! The expanding park won various awards. The Hortons then decided to design their own caravans based on American designs and christened them 'mobile homes', as they could be moved to another plot if needed. The 'Pathfinder Ten Wide' was built by Willerby and special pitches were laid for them. By the end of the 1950s the Hortons

FUN FACT

If your site opened in mid March, then you might expect cold spells. With less insulation in caravans back then, after a cold frosty night you could wake up half-frozen with ice forming on the interior panels of the caravan. If no fire was fitted you had to put the cooker on for warmth.

were constructing caravans in their own workshop on-site. The Pathfinder range subsequently began to be sold to other sites, a dedicated factory was built, and today Pathfinder brand is well known as a builder of luxury lodges.

With homes up to 11m length now coming out of some of the big-name factories, transport was becoming even more of a challenge. Although, the early 1950s idea of joining caravans with a central corridor hadn't proved popular, two 7m lengths that could more easily be transported and then be joined up on site seemed an obvious solution to the problem and was tried once more. Bessacarr, a Yorkshire-based manufacturer, created several models that were joined in the middle. Marston, Paladin, Bluebird and Berkeley would also exploit this idea for the living van, with the idea carrying on from the early '50s to the early '60s, though site owners increasingly found that caravans over 12m long were difficult to accommodate. The idea of joining two halves together to make a chalet/bungalow did have some success, though. Premier Caravans (part of Bluebird) launched their successful Bungalow along with Bluebird's Swedish Cottage. Lissett also went this way, and Paladin produced the very successful Sun Cottage – which was also sold to London councils to provide additional housing in the prevailing climate of accommodation shortages.

Pathfinder 10 wide home on the Pathfinder mobile home site at Pathfinder village near Exeter around 1960. Note the side porches, designed to give a domestic look.

A Revolutionary Idea in Caravans!

IT WIDENS AS YOU WIND!

A new era has opened in British caravans. Gone for good are cramped conditions and tiny living space. The accent now is on spaciousness—on sizeable bedrooms—big wide living quarters—a roomy kitchen in fact, more space everywhere to add maximum comfort to caravan life.   And leading the way in this long-overdue trend is a sensational new trailer—the widest mobile home in the world—the magnificent "Deeside de Luxe."

The "Deeside" on the road—only 7ft. 6in. wide

EARLY 50% WIDER *than any other Caravan!*

Right: Premier Caravans of Bristol launched its forward-thinking Bungalow twin unit in 1960, ahead of the Bluebird Swedish Cottage and the Paladin Sun Cottage in 1962.

Left: The unique Deeside holiday/living caravan. Once sited it could be widened from 2.3m to 3.22m using a winding handle.

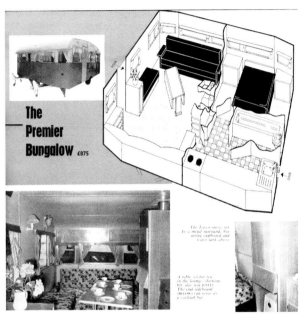

The Premier Bungalow £875

As the 1960s progressed the static caravan lost its traditional caravan shape and began to look more like a unit designed only ever to be moved once or twice. These design changes began to create a separate identity for the static holiday caravan. Makes such as Lynton, Summerdale, Willerby, Fairview, Wonderland and Bluebird all designed new profiles which were modern and more suited for permanent use. Pemberton were also producing new looking static caravans with distinctive body shapes while in 1963 they

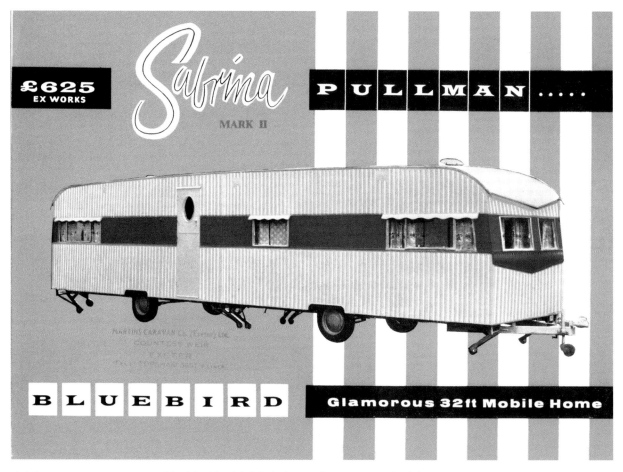

Joining two caravans, as with this Bluebird Sabrina Pullman, was ideal for transportation but took up large plots on sites.

had made their Mustang model wider at 2.92m and offering excellent value for money. By the mid 1960s they had developed a distinctive look both inside and out, making it easy to spot a Pemberton on site. The first dedicated caravan and static caravan show was held at Earls Court in 1960, generating great interest in static caravans and the increasingly modern styling. *Mobile Home* magazine was launched in late 1959, and is still going in 2019 as *Park Home and Holiday Caravan*, now under Kelsey Publications. As it did from the start, this magazine keeps both trade and public up to date with

Memories

Mike Parker:

I loved static caravans; my parents would hire one at Newton Hall Caravan Park, Staining. By the early '60s my parents bought a new Dovedale Monarch on the site. In fact with Pemberton's I loved the Dovedale brand for their designs plus they were also made at Blackpool. The site had a bar and bingo nights too, and as a small boy I would go around Newton Hall looking at the different makes and styles. Pure nostalgia. I still look back to those glorious times with my family.

Mike Parker, age 12, in 1961 with his parents' Dovedale Monarch. (Courtesy of Mike Parker)

the latest news on homes and new sites and models, so proved useful to owners and would-be owners of holiday and park homes.

A major change on sites was the increasing provision of proper toilet blocks and showers, though most holiday statics had a utility room and chemical toilet. All cooking and lighting was now on gas, and the solid stove was to give way to the gas fire as dedicated manufacturers incorporated these into their static designs. The touring caravan pitches were also being moved away from static pitches, though some tourers continued to be used in a similar capacity to statics in the 1950s and '60s.

High demand for static holiday caravans in the late 1950s saw factories such as Pemberton's working 24–7.

The booming '50s had seen caravan sites expand. Ownership of a car meant that a weekend away to your favourite destination – perhaps a caravan site – was easy. The static caravan in particular was growing in popularity, with sales soaring higher than ever in the 1960s. Demand was for affordable statics, both

Some static owners found private land to put their unit on, as with this Coventry Steel. Owners would let it to friends and relatives.

for individual owners and also site owners who were buying bulk statics to feed the demand for hiring. Neither party wanted super luxury units; they wanted cheap vans that could sleep a family in comfort with a cooker and gas lighting; they needed little else, as the caravans were intended for summer use only. Small landowners were also getting in on the act, obtaining permission for one or two statics on their land and hiring them out for summer holidays. Often they would buy second-hand models from larger sites, though some of these caravans left a lot to be desired. High demand meant that folk wouldn't turn their noses up at them, though – a holiday was all they wanted.

Memories

Andrew Jenkinson:

I remember a week's holiday in Scotland with my best friend and his parents. This would have been around 1966/67. As young children we wanted to camp but his parents found a small two-caravan site behind a house. We called in by chance and yes a static caravan was available but for only a few days. From distant memory they were '50s Willerby caravans with old-style gaslights and a spartan interior. But although they had seen better days my friend and I thought it a big adventure. I can still hear the hissing of gas lights and taste beans on toast.

The caravan boom was not only happening in the UK but in Europe too. MG Caravans was ahead of the game in the 1960s, helping to establish sites out in France by transporting UK vans there to be sited and hired out. With European caravan manufacturing being less developed, and prices favourable, UK makers were soon struggling to keep up with export demand.

Some smaller low volume makes also went out of business as mass production came to dominate; the static caravan was to be produced in larger factories. Some of the more established players endured but were struggling. Paladin would stop manufacturing holiday statics and mobile homes in 1967 and go into portable building manufacture. Berkeley also suffered, as a result of Panter's attempted move into the sports car business with the Berkeley car. He had been pouring the firm's profits into this new venture, but the fibreglass body shells were costly, and with sales poor and rows of cars sitting in storage, Berkeley went bust in 1960.

Astral was another new Hull maker that exported large amounts of holiday/mobile homes such as this Westwood 1963 static holiday home.

Panter was soon back up and running, but with stiffer competition in the caravan industry Berkeley would fold again by 1962. Marston and Normandie had also called it a day as the newer makers forged ahead.

Others, old and new, were finding their own ways to compete. Pemberton, for instance, which had just launched its new-look range, was offering the workforce bonus payments to achieve its high targets. Thomson Caravans, the big Scottish maker, had begun to produce large, coach-style living vans, but wouldn't get into proper holiday home production and design until the early '70s. Donnington and Dorchester would go into mobile home manufacture, leaving tourers and static holiday

The 1969 Travelmaster Gemini showed how far the mobile home had come in the last decade, with fashionable fittings and domestic-sized kitchens.

Pleszko, founder of Omar, which would become a very successful company by the late '60s.

caravans, while Travelmaster at Princess Risborough also moved from the holiday and tourer market to mobile homes with some very impressive designs. Using all the latest furniture and soft furnishing trends the interiors of the Travelmasters were modern and very practical.

The 1960s saw the emergence of new makers, one being Omar, a park home manufacturer still in business today. Omar was founded in 1961, but not under that name till 1964. Its founder, Mr. K Pleszko, had been in the Polish Army. After leaving in 1950 and marrying, he built his first mobile home. By 1964 the Omar brand was producing its 8m-long holiday lodge, which would put the company firmly on the map. Other models quickly followed, and Omar's innovative new construction ideas made the company one of the most prestigious.

Colonial, based near Blackpool, was heavily influenced by US mobile home design. After a visit to the States, founder Bob Greenhalgh decided that the US had

The Omar Holiday Lodge, launched 1964, used cedarwood on part of the exterior.

THE 1950S AND 1960S 69

it right. He even bought a big American car. He named his mobile homes the Texan range, and they were large, twin-axled 36ft monsters. His brother, based at Bispham, originally launched his own Skyline brand, but merged with his brother in 1963, dropping the Skyline as a brand name.

In Wales, Stately Homes was founded in 1964. The company would come to be known for its quality mobile homes, including the Gem, Consort, Monarch and Domain De-Luxe. The company grew quickly, becoming a top park home manufacturer by the 1980s.

The new mobile homes had to have all mod cons. Makes such as Kenkast Homes would thus enter the market. Based in Manchester, Kenkast was a sectional building specialist, using mock brick corners to give its mobile homes a bungalow appearance. By the '60s, Davan, a pre-war maker, was making mobile homes to order. The public could not get enough of static holidays and the mobile home was also proving popular with the retired as well as newly-weds.

FUN FACT

Workers at the Skyline factory were proud to wheel out their first 40ft mobile home. As they admired the unit a cracking sound was heard. The home had split in the middle bending the chassis. It was back to the drawing board!

Fairview Caravans formed by the Hammerton family in the early '50s had produced holiday statics with rear door entry and the Harwich based company would become a strong force in mobile homes. The mid 1960s onwards would see successful models launched, such as the Ganges, Hudson, Rhine and Missouri. With distinctive profiles and interiors, Fairview

Fairview produced some good designs, such as this 1964 Ganges holiday model.

sold well – but the next decade would see the company's demise.

By the end of the '50s, manufacturers such as Robin Caravans and Astral had joined Willerby Caravans in the Hull area. Willerby would acquire Robin Caravans and also Acklam twin homes to get into this market sector in the '60s. Astral, the big Hull timber importer owned by the Spooner family, entered caravan production in 1959 and within a few years had moved into a new larger factory. Astral made tourers but also popular holiday models such as Gaytime, Westwood, Clearview and Classic.

Also based in Hull were new makers Silverline, run by the Robinson family. Silverline specialised in what was to be termed towable static holiday caravans – caravans at 6.7m that could be pulled by a large vehicle. Towable statics became quite popular from the 1960s and into the '70s. A-Line Caravans, originally Alpine Coachcraft, was purchased by David Wilkinson in 1968. The Wilkinsons would make A-Line one of the biggest manu-facturers of caravans and static holiday homes in the Hull area, alongside Astral.

Another new Hull maker was Belmont Caravans, which in 1964 launched the Havana. It looked very much like an Astral static, but this new company soon had brimming order books and export orders too. Belmont would grow, increasing its ranges and providing stiff competition for both Pemberton and Bluebird. By the end of the 1960s it had moved its factory to Swinemoor Lane, Beverley – a stone's throw from another new company, Ace Caravans, a maker of popular tourers who were soon to begin making towable statics. As we will see in the next chapter, these two neighbours would soon have a common goal.

The big name in this period, however, was Bluebird. The company had become

21ft x 8ft · 25¼ cwt · 4 Berth

PRICE
£550
EX-WORKS

Silverline

PULMAN PRINCE

This model is specially designed as a touring caravan or residential Mobile Home and accommodates 4 people in up-to-the-minute comfort. The lounge has large panoramic windows, ample seating facilities with 6" deep interior sprung mattresses and cushion, free standing drop leaf table, generous sized wardrobes (one with fitted shelves), double doors open out to partition off lounge, sideboard, locker space and airing cupboard completes the furnishings.

The kitchenette comprises ample floor locker space, deep sink with drainer, super quality cooker (storage under) and overhead lockers. The end bedroom contains double bed with headboard, dressing table and wardrobe.

Carpet fitted in lounge.

Calor gas lighting.

New type of calor gas heating system installed giving convected heat for less than 2d. an hour.

Specification: The body is soundly constructed with first class timber. The exterior appearance is the same as the Princess model. The van is fully insulated. 22 SWG Aluminium covers the exterior. Boat-shaped roof. Inside headroom 6' 8½". Stable type door. Calor gas floor socket. Peaks full braking chassis. Oak furniture in lounge, kitchen and bedroom.

We reserve the right to alter or amend the price or specification without prior notice.

SILVERLINE CARAVAN CO. LTD.
Head Office **PULMAN STREET, SPRING BANK WEST, HULL.**   Tel. Hull 55906

Hull makers Silverline developed the Pullman Prince for holiday or residential use.

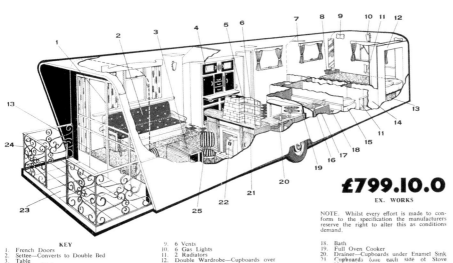

£799.10.0

EX. WORKS

NOTE. Whilst every effort is made to conform to the specification the manufacturers reserve the right to alter this as conditions demand.

KEY

1. French Doors
2. Settee—Converts to Double Bed
3. Table
4. Kitchen Cabinet
5. Decorative Stone Chimney Breast
6. Tiled Kitchenette
7. 3 Roof Lights
8. Corner Dressing Table—Mirror above
9. 6 Vents
10. 6 Gas Lights
11. 2 Radiators
12. Double Wardrobe—Cupboards over
13. Carpets
14. Built-in Linen Cupboard—Wardrobes
15. Single Bed—Single Bunk over
16. Hot and Cold Taps
17. Toilet under Basin
18. Bath
19. Full Oven Cooker
20. Drainer—Cupboards under Enamel Sink
21. Cupboards (one each side of Stove Housing)
22. Hard Fuel Stove, Boiler back
23. Tiled Patio
24. Wrought-Iron Patio Rail
25. 2 Striped Chairs

KEY FLOOR PLAN

A. Double Wardrobe, Cupboards over
B. Double Bed
C. Built-in Wardrobes
D. Single Bed and Single Bunk over
E. Bath
F. Wash Basin, Toilet under
G. Full Oven Cooker
H. Kitchen Cabinet
I. Hard Fuel Stove, Boiler back
J. Drainer, Cupboards under Enamel Sink
K. Settee–Double Bed
L. Gateleg Table
M. Patio
N. Shelves and Cupboards
O. Striped Chairs

SPECIFICATION

Shell of external aluminium panelling and roof, with interior walls of hardboard; insulated throughout with Fibreglass. Framing of $1\frac{1}{2}$in. x $\frac{3}{4}$in. timbers, half-jointed and screwed, door frames $1\frac{1}{2}$in. x $1\frac{1}{2}$in. Flooring of $\frac{1}{2}$in. plywood, carried on 22 wood cross bearers 4in. x $1\frac{1}{2}$in. Chassis has two channel steel longitudinal bearers 4in. x $1\frac{1}{2}$in. x $\frac{1}{4}$in., steel angle cross members 2in. x 2in. x 3/16in., with cantilever side supports built up from $1\frac{1}{2}$in. x $1\frac{1}{2}$in. x $\frac{1}{4}$in. steel angle members. Folding platform at front 9ft. x 4ft. Automatic coupling. Screwdown corner jacks. Heavy duty undergear; pressed-steel wheels with 750 x 16 heavy duty tyres. External colourings in grey and ivory with red doors and window frames.   Dimensions : Length 30ft. Width 9ft. 6in.

Bluebird's Pacific home was designed with the help of site owners Allens in 1962. This is the king-size version.

PEOPLE WHO KNOW LIVE IN THE NEW
TEXAN

36 FT. TEXAN SINGLE UNIT AT £875 0. 0. Ex Works

STANDARD PLAN (CHOICE OF SEVERAL LAYOUTS)

THIS SECTION AVAILABLE IN ALTERNATIVE LAYOUTS

CAN ACCOMMODATE UP TO TEN PEOPLE IN COMFORT !

Above: Site owners Allens built the US-influenced Retreat from 1965. Sales were limited due to a large plot being required.

Left: Colonial Caravans were strongly influenced by American mobile home design; the Texan 36 could sleep up to ten.

a giant and was now under Bluebird Investments after going public. Knott was in a big position of power, with his Bluebird factory buying in large amounts of raw materials at prices other manufacturers could rarely beat.

Bluebird launched its Pacific, an American-influenced model designed for permanent living; it was a joint venture with expanding dealer and site owner Allen's. In the early 1960s they had begun manufacturing caravans for their own sites. They were influenced by US design. Their American Retreat, a mobile home with large side windows, required special plots to accommodate its 11.5m length and 3.04m width. But by 1965 Allen's had ceased manufacturing.

Meanwhile, Sprite Caravans at Newmarket had also expanded rapidly under owner Sam Alper. He and Knott had always been rivals, but Knott wasn't about to give up his number one spot. In 1960 Eccles caravans sold out to Sprite, and for a few years several holiday homes were produced, but by 1962 that stopped. The acquisition gave Alper the same buying power as Knott, however, and gradually companies such as Paladin and Berkeley would fall behind.

In 1963 the merger of Bluebird and Sprite/Eccles Ltd was announced. Alper was chairman while Knott ducked out with a few quid in his back pocket. The deal was that Knott was not allowed to manufacturer caravans for two years. This cooling off period suited Knott, as he began development on a new brand of static caravans – more on that shortly.

Now with Sprite Eccles and Bluebird, Alper had the biggest caravan manufacturing business in the world; a new parent company was formed to encompass the three brands, Caravans International or Ci. The new company was the culmination of Alper's ambition. In fifteen years he had come from manufacturing one caravan a week to around 400.

With such a formidable force at his disposal Alper invested money into

Eccles concentrated on tourers in the 1960s, although the Emerald, classed as a towable static, was often seen permanently sited.

new production methods, and also into developing new models. From the mid 1960s, Bluebird Static Caravans would become a top-selling range with modern exteriors and interiors to match, yet prices remained sensible.

By the late 1960s Bluebird had some superb designs, mainly mobile homes intended for young newly-weds to buy as they saved for bricks and mortar. The Guardian was one of the company's most popular models with its modern looks as a building with veranda and side porch. Many residential sites had Bluebird Guardians, Vanguards and Vulcans.

Bluebird's 1968 brochure actively encouraged the buyer of a Bluebird to seriously think about letting out their pride and joy! Why not just use it for a few weekends, said the brochure, and hire it out for summer and make an income courtesy of Bluebird!

Eccles, meanwhile, also a Ci brand, was making the Emerald, a towable static 7m

Sam Alper OBE of Sprite Eccles. His merger with Bluebird formed Ci, the biggest caravan company in the world.

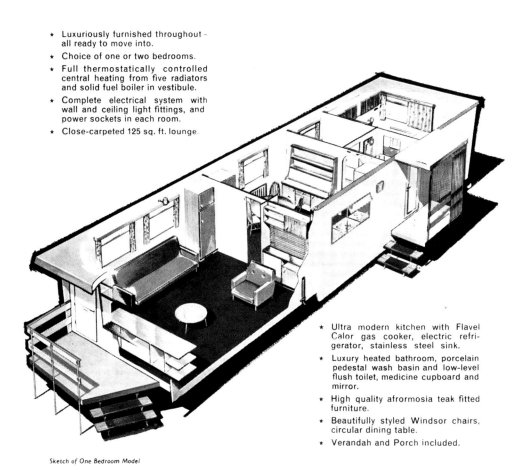

* ★ Luxuriously furnished throughout – all ready to move into.
* ★ Choice of one or two bedrooms.
* ★ Full thermostatically controlled central heating from five radiators and solid fuel boiler in vestibule.
* ★ Complete electrical system with wall and ceiling light fittings, and power sockets in each room.
* ★ Close-carpeted 125 sq. ft. lounge.

* ★ Ultra modern kitchen with Flavel Calor gas cooker, electric refrigerator, stainless steel sink.
* ★ Luxury heated bathroom, porcelain pedestal wash basin and low-level flush toilet, medicine cupboard and mirror.
* ★ High quality afrormosia teak fitted furniture.
* ★ Beautifully styled Windsor chairs, circular dining table.
* ★ Verandah and Porch included.

Sketch of One Bedroom Model

After Bluebird became part of Ci more modern designs emerged from the new team of designers. The Vanguard proved especially popular.

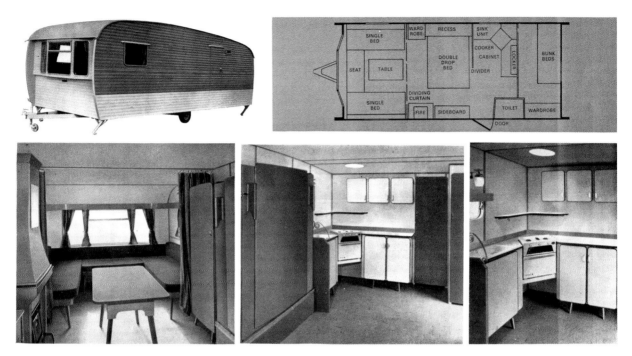

Pemberton's 1968 Sunstar. With their distinctive profile and practical interior, Pembertons were easy to spot on site.

in length that could sleep up to six people. The modern interior, typical of caravan designer Reg Dean, made a popular run from 1962 to 1970. By 1969 Sprite had dropped its static caravan manufacturing to concentrate on Sprite tourers. Ci also bought out Wilk/Stern in Germany and Fairholme in Cardiff.

There was competition, however, in the form of Bill Knott's new venture, BK.

Knott set his new firm up in Poole and began manufacturing holiday caravans. By 1967 his Britannia range also included two mobile homes. Knott concentrated on offering value and quality at the right price.

Other names in the '60s included Lyndhurst Mobile Homes, Ercall, Mardon, Cosalt-Abbey Caravans, Jayge, Gold Star, Sovereign, Aaro, Belmont, Ace, Minerva and Albatross.

From 1960 to 1970 the static caravan was now looking more bungalow in design; but the caravan name still stuck. Sites were becoming more organised with cut grass plots, hard standing and toilet blocks. In the early 1960s sites were founded by a few caravans with no hassle from planners, but new laws were brought in to keep check on sites. The '60s saw static holiday caravans become larger and more sophisticated in their design. Static's had got wider and longer, with mobile homes following the same trend. Both increasingly tended to have their gas heating and mains electricity installed. Both individual ownership and the hire market expanded greatly. There were also more sites being owned by a group, bringing several sites under one umbrella and upgrading standards in the process.

The '60s ended on a high, with sites booming and sales of both statics and mobile homes climbing. The next decade would see a peak in sales followed a massive dip as the economy suffered in the mid '70s, taking several large companies down. It was to be a volatile period, but the UK industry mostly rode the storm.

Opposite: Bluebird's brochure was designed to sell the static holiday caravan lifestyle and offer advice on hiring out your investment.

BLUEBIRD HOLIDAY HOMES

superb — every model an investment!

JUNE 1960

Every two months   Two shillings

MOBILE HOME

The first journal of the caravan home

Mobile Home magazine was dedicated to the holiday market too, and would be renamed *Park Home & Holiday Caravan* years later.

Memories

Martin Greenwood, owner of MG Caravans, one of the UK's oldest dealerships, grew up with tourers and statics:

My grandad used to tow a towable static up to Scotland and site it on a plot of land then rent out the caravan. He would take around six static caravans where they would be placed for years. But it wasn't just the UK because we used to go to the South of France too delivering caravans to hire on site. I and my brother had great times in the school holidays always going somewhere having great adventures, those times were very happy ones.

Martin (right) and Michael Greenwood in 1961 with their 1950s Berkeley Caravan and Land Rover. (Courtesy of Martin Greenwood)

PARTINGTONS HOLIDAY CENTRES

INDY HARBOUR
RAVAN & HOLIDAY CENTRE
GLETON PARK Nr. BLACKPOOL

NEWTON HAL
CARAVAN & HOLIDAY CENTI
STAINING ROAD BLACKPOO

ROADWATER
RAVAN & HOLIDAY CENTRE
FLEETWOOD

BALLYFERRI
CARAVAN & HOLIDAY CENTR
BALLYFERRIS Nr. Belfast N. Irelar
PROP. THORNROLD DEVELOPMEN

Site businesses were growing, offering more to owners and hirers; they produced brochures such as this one from the mid '60s.

3 The 1970s and 1980s

The 1970s and '80s would witness a surge in leisure time, with more choices of holiday than ever before. The package holiday, with sunshine almost guaranteed, proved popular. Prices had come down, making a trip to Spain and the rest of Europe even more enticing. Timeshares, villas and holiday cottages were becoming more and more popular too. Would this be the end of the boom in static caravans? With stiff competition in the leisure industry, site owners would further invest to upgrade facilities to lure folk to their sites – now often described as 'caravan parks'. Manufacturers would also have to up their game to with new designs and features.

The boom in sales of the late 1960s certainly continued into the early part of the '70s. Seaside parks were still popular, and with ever bigger hire fleets owned by the site owners more folk were introduced into static caravan holidays and eventually ownership. With parks now beginning to

Outdoor swimming pools at caravan parks were becoming more common in the 1970s, to pull in the crowds. (Courtesy of Holgates)

Parks by the sea proved ever more popular, especially with families.

open for longer periods, the static holiday vans offered better value for both owners and hirers.

The mobile home market was also on the up, as the idea of retiring to a mobile home with money left over to bank was alluring. Married couples who didn't want to rent would find purchasing a mobile home was easier, with easy payment terms. Another bonus was that they came

Memories

Mike Parker:

I decided to go into the static holiday hire caravan business; I began in around 1974 buying a Pemberton. Soon I expanded my units, which were on the then newly-opened Marton Mere Caravan Park and Newton Hall Holiday Park. I built up a small fleet, replacing them over the years with new models from Pemberton, Jayge, Galaxy, Blue Anchor, Aaro, Cosalt and A-Line. I had a good run into the '80s and mid '90s, with hardly a week without a hire. Site fees, though, began to climb and I gave it up due to rising costs, but I enjoyed doing it.

One of Mike Parkers hire statics in the late '70s. Subletting, as it was called, was common in this period.

ready furnished, and most had all the facilities of bricks and mortar. By the 1980s there were plenty of parks catering exclusively for retired folk, though the hire purchase squeeze from the early 1970s had no doubt restrained some of the buying public from purchasing a static holiday model or mobile home.

Ci had, at the end of the '60s moved into caravan parks, growing the static side of the industry. Bluebird static holiday homes could be usually found a plot onto a Ci owned park. With smaller companies struggling to get plots, the public wouldn't order and small manufacturers would finish production. By 1972 though Ci had sold its parks side and commented that they had entered park ownership to prove that an upgraded well-run park would be an example to park owners to up their game.

Ci was also innovating in other ways. In 1971 it used its Bluebird division to come up with a new concept called the Mini Motel. It was based on the same

Bluebirds Mini Motel chalet-styled unit was very adaptable, but it didn't catch on.

construction of its Static holiday homes but an upgraded construction could be ordered. It was designed to be used as an office, as extra accommodation on private land, or even as part of a chalet park. All the unit needed was a level concrete base. The idea was to provide an instantly useable building. Bathroom, beds, a desk and a veranda were all part of the design. The idea didn't take off. Swift Group launched a similar idea named the S Pod, to greater success, in 2016.

The big manufacturers were experimenting with new materials. Aluminium exteriors were the norm, with cedar planking also being used by firms such as Omar, Nene Valley and Fairview. New exterior finishes were looked at and tried to offer the buyer more choices. Omar was ahead in its thinking by late 1969, using injected polyurethane foam into the sides and ends which gave solid walls and superb insulation. Silverline would also use this method from 1971 right up to the company's last static

produced in 1983, while Willerby also used sandwich construction for 1980 with its Manhattan. Plastic-coated steel and zinc-coated sheets named 'Stelvetite' emerged and were used by such companies as Pemberton and Belmont. Pemberton combined this with a new profile for 1972. The new look again gave Pemberton easy to spot features while interiors remained as practical as ever. Boasting they were still the top static holiday home producers, Pemberton's three factories were working flat out in the early 1970s.

Belmont's San Capello and the more popular San Tropez Villa range in 1972/3 could be had as residential use or as a luxury eight-berth holiday static. They had mock woodgrain exterior finish, and their shape copied a typical chalet design, so they were also easy to spot on a park!

The static holiday home as well as the mobile home manufacturer was always looking at methods of different construction for their models with new finishes. The fact that many static

Sunflower '72   £645 ex works

The Sunflower '72—a six berth caravan with sleeping accommodation comprising two single bed settees, a combination dinette double bed, and two bunk beds in the childrens bedroom. An attractive gas fire provides "all-round" heating in the roomy lounge which is part carpeted and contains a wardrobe, an elegant sideboard, and a large feature mirror. Complimenting this tastily designed room is a newly featured panoramic picture window allowing the wood grain finish and warm furnishings to be shown at their best. The large side windows are of the opening type permitting maximum ventilation. There is an oven cooker and sink unit in the compact kitchen which has ample drawer and cupboard space and good working surfaces.

22' × 9' 6"

Pemberton was the biggest static maker. New exterior designs for 1972 and construction were headline news. The Sunflower could sleep six.

SAN CAPELLO

SAN TROPEZ

The newly formed Ace Belmont International invested heavily in new designs, such as these two chalet-style holiday statics.

caravans and mobile homes were made by caravan manufacturers had meant that getting away from the caravan image had proved difficult. But as designs improved, particularly with the development of with twin units, the caravan influence was slowly fading. A-Line by 1980 had produced some very stylish statics and a good range too. But a mobile home was still seen as the best a way to have your own home if you were just married and couldn't get a house.

At the start of the 1970s, newcomers of the 1960s, such as Wonderland, were moving quickly. Wonderland founder Ron Smith was formerly of Bluebird Caravans. He had left Bluebird after the Ci formation and set up a factory at old brickworks in Okeford Fitzpaine, Dorset, producing Wonderlands. Smith had redeveloped the site and now had a factory that also produced special units for companies. By 1970 they were adding new cladding to

Memories

Phil and Carole Whitmore:

Gosh it seems so long ago! We had just got married in 1975 and found houses a little expensive so we went to a dealer, Newark Caravans, who ordered us our choice, a Bluebird Vanguard. We loved our mobile home and when the children came along we decided it was time to buy a house. We loved that life and when we retired a few years ago we purchased a new park home although light years ahead of the Bluebird we had.

their Wonderland homes with Honeyex, a material used for buildings in Japan.

Ercall was another late 1960s mobile home producer. A small Shropshire company, it could produce only a few units a month. Ercall wanted to produce a chalet/cottage twin unit and designed a unit that was more like a bungalow, getting away from the holiday caravan image. They let customers choose their own decor and ideas, while sizes ranged from 28ft x 16ft to 40ft x 20ft. The company built a large range of portable buildings and was part of the Powys Group of companies. Kenkast, who were a sectional building manufacturer, had by the early '70s proved successful with their mobile homes with their imitation stone block exterior corners already mentioned.

Bill Knott who had steered Bluebird's success had founded BK Caravans in 1964/1965 at Parkstone, Poole, not far

A-Line had become a large manufacturer by the late 1970s, and by 1980 produced some interesting designs.

. . . with the luxury look for the asking!

Your Wonderland will really look its best in Honeyex exterior cladding—pleasant to touch, good to look at—and extra insulation, too. It's available as an optional extra on all Wonderland residential models.

Wonderland launched its Woodland mobile home with new branded exterior cladding, Honeyex. It was optional on all other models.

from the Bluebird factory. Knott aimed at value with his holiday statics and mobile homes building up a following at home and abroad. By 1974 it had three ranges of models: Popular, Trident and Britannia. Keen prices were key as were lengths from 6m designed to tempt buyers with limited funds in the mid-1970s recession and high inflation costs. In 1975 you could buy a Popular 19 for £932. BK's low prices suited the hire fleet buyers as well as the public. Pemberton tried the same tactic with its Mercury, which was a foot longer and £33 more, while in 1974 Astral hit the market with the 500, which cost just £833.

Although DIY caravan building had become a fading pastime, Stephenson Developments (who had been involved with Summerdale Caravans in 1967) manufactured what was essentially a flat-pack holiday home chalet that you could assemble on a concrete plot and connect to a mains supply. The idea had little success, with folk preferring a factory-built unit, so few were sold.

New company Jayge was founded in late 1968 by ex Nene Valley director Jack Goodlife, who had left Nene Valley after USA based Divico Wayne took over. Goodlife saw a gap in the market for a static holiday range, and followed this up a year or two later with a range of mobile homes. In his time with Nene Valley coachworks Goodlife had amassed plenty of experience in the industry. His ranges Clipper, Clipper Home and Sunsea Chaletvan were soon to be well established in the static holiday home market.

Tourer manufacturers Fleetwind near Preston would in 1972 enter the static holiday market (they began in 1968 with tourers) with two eight-berth models designed to capture the hire market. The company would expand its line up and exports would prove to be a strong market. In fact, UK static holiday homes were in high demand across Europe with many UK makers only producing static holiday vans for export markets.

Bill Knott's BK brand quickly caught buyers' imaginations. Knott's designs offered value and durability.

Hailed by site operators and weekenders alike as the most exciting newcomers to static caravans, the Fleetwind range is extended further for 1973 by the addition of a new Model 20

Fleetwind Caravans began manufacturing statics alongside its tourers in 1972. The company produced a range of static units till 1980.

The 1970s would still see many caravan parks have loo blocks, many still not having statics plumbed in. It was also a time when park owners would spread their wings and buy up other parks making small and large groups. Caravan parks were still growing. Brothers John and Arthur Woodward built up their park portfolio on the Lincolnshire coast, eventually owning eight holiday static parks. They added to this by going into static holiday home production in the summer of 1970. Named Blue Anchor Caravans, their company produced the Parkland home range with distinctive blue waist band on the exterior and rosewood finish furniture with orange plastic glazed sliding locker doors. The staple gun was much in evidence in construction to keep costs down and by 1971 a new factory was built producing seventy units a week. With a big Dutch order for £5 million Blue Anchor quickly established itself,

Blue Anchor launched in 1970, and its Parkland range expanded over the years. It no longer produces holiday homes, but has fourteen parks today.

particularly for the fleet hire business on larger parks.

The 1970s also saw the birth of Tingdene Homes. The Northants company would soon make a big impact on the market with it US-influenced designs, such as its Villa model. Tingdene would further grow over the years getting involved with park ownership, acquiring three parks by 1998.

Manufacturers continued to flourish in Hull and the surrounding areas. New names included Avalon, Apollo, Volnay, Rivera, Beverley Coachcraft, Stag and Castle, while Belmont Caravans moved to a new factory at Swinemoor Lane Beverley in late 1971, where Ace caravans had also set up shop. Making statics as well as tourers, Ace had begun to attract big orders. Belmont too had swelling order books. Both large concerns by 1972, they announced a merger to become the second-largest caravan manufacturer in

Fancy a DIY holiday chalet? Nobody else did either, and the idea flopped in the early 1970s.

Ace produced tourers, and by 1970 statics as well. Pictured is the 1971 8.22m eight-berth Aristocrat, which cost £809.

the UK, second only to Ci Group. Named Ace Belmont International (ABI), it would overtake A Line, Thomson and Astral. Ace had begun to also gain a following with site operators, so the Ace name would continue to be used for the new company's static holiday homes until 1980.

The exploding market had at one period become confusing for buyers of static units. Problems were arising with used static holiday caravans with demand falling in the early '70s, with buyers wanting the more modern well-planned and more fashionable decors. Some owners did hang on to their late '50s and early '60s holiday homes, but by the late '80s some parks wanted rid of these old and poorly-maintained units that looked unsightly.

Lynton led the way when it came to the change in styles, in particular with its Beachcomber chalet. Lynton's design flair had come from Reg Dean who had worked for Ci Group, redesigning the 1962 Eccles touring range using white vinyl walls with teakwood locker doors; interiors followed the latest trends in decor. Dean left Ci, much to the annoyance of Sam Alper, to join Manchester-based Lynton. Dean

Lynton's 1971 Beachcomber was trendy inside and out, typical of Reg Dean's flair in design; he later worked for ABI and A-Line.

The interior of the Lynton was contemporary and spacious. Dean used the latest trends at Lynton.

shook up the ranges, and by 1971 Lynton produced the most stylish tourer/static holiday caravan interiors in the UK. The Beachcomber emulated a modern seaside chalet. A verandah-style porch cost £31 extra to the price of the £815 Golden Beachcomber but the Lyntons were very modern for their time.

Park owners would find it difficult to find pitches, and mobile home users were seeing fewer sales as bricks-and-mortar prices remained stable. The NCC pushed for new parks with the government, proving the advantages of instant housing and how parks could be progressed to be placed near amenities and also be well managed.

Willerby, Pemberton and Bluebird remained household names in statics and mobile homes but Blue Anchor, ABI and A Line were catching up.

A flooded market saw some makers such as Travelmaster, Fairview and Paladin, all respected names, cease production; increased competition meant sales were

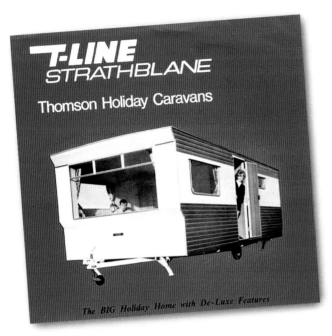

Big Scottish tourer company Thomson produced holiday statics from the early 1970s; this is the 1973 Strathblane model.

spread more thinly, even in boom time. Fairview owners the Hammerton brothers (once a park owner) would still be involved with the industry in that respect and also started up FC luxury tourers in 1973.

Scottish maker Thomson entered back into holiday static caravans in 1972 after a few years previously purchasing land at Kingcraig in Scotland to develop parks. Thomsons' statics didn't sell as the company expected, and production was very much stop and go, but they made five models till the firm's demise in early 1982.

Manufacturers of statics and mobile homes factories were always at high risk of fires. Smoking was allowed in most cases, and, although by the late 1960s real veneer furniture had given way to cheaper more durable photo-finish materials, fires were not unheard of. Willerby suffered in September 1970, resulting in a halt in the production of its 1971 models. Apollo Caravans, a relatively new maker, also suffered a major fire at their Beverley plant when a neighbouring factory's fire spread to theirs.

With factories working flat out and park owners investing into adding mains services to some holiday pitches as well as residential, the boom continued.

Factory fires were quite common; this is Apollo's one Friday afternoon in 1975, and the factory was gutted. (Image courtesy of Carnaby Homes)

Then came disaster. The oil crisis hit, and in April 1973 VAT was added to tourers and holiday caravans plus components. Inflation would rise, and the three-day week struck. Sales slowed and by late 1973 factories had cut back or closed. Albatross, a big name, shut its doors, but its Mallards Close factory would be reorganised by ex-Albatross personnel with Brentmere Holiday Homes emerging. Park owners were left with half-finished projects. Some would push on hoping for a lift in the gloom. Borrowing cost was higher than it had been, which slowed hire purchase

Memories

Andrew Crates:

In 1973 my grandparents purchased a then new Belmont Pasadena at Newbeach Holiday Centre Dymchurch Kent. The 8.22m Belmont was one of the first on the park to have mains water, electrics and a loo! Grandad decided to add a porch so he made one himself and with his trailer took sections down each weekend before assembling it. I can remember going home in Essex on a Friday after school excited at a weekend in the van... since then I have loved the static holiday home!

Andrew Crates's grandparents' 1973 Belmont with home-made porch. Andrew had many happy holidays at Newbeach in Kent.

homes in Spain, mainly purchased by UK retirees as second homes. Galaxy at first exported built units to the parks, but demand was high and Galaxy struggled to keep up supply so instead it began to

Preston-based Galaxy Celeste from 1977, the start of a popular run of ranges for the firm.

sales. However, exports remained stable, keeping many manufacturers afloat, and some, such as Astral, Aaro and Silverline, even received Queen's Awards for Export achievements during this period.

From early 1976, Galaxy Mobile Homes, a Preston-based company, began prototyping its new range of static holiday caravans. They produced up to ten units a week, with orders coming in from as far as Scandinavia. The company would expand its portfolio, producing affordable quality static holiday caravans. The company also spotted a lucrative market for mobile

ship them out in kit form, sending a team from the factory to assemble them at the park. Galaxy would become one of the top sellers in statics and also would later produce twelve wide models by 1985. Other companies copied their business model of sending holiday caravans abroad, such as Omar with its 7m-long Concertina holiday home.

By 1975 things had picked up, and some tourer manufacturers would dabble into the static holiday market, Forrest and Boomerang being two major examples. Sovereign and Mardon also concentrated on statics, cutting tourer production.

Other tourer manufacturers like Minster, Mardon, Sovereign, Lunar, and luxury tourer maker Royale (Fiesta) and Riviera would also make statics in the early '70s. ABI had found success with statics as with its tourers, and the choice to the buyer was as bewildering as ever. A Line had several ranges of holiday statics covering all price bands.

Blue Anchor was the same along with all the manufacturers as they tried to cover all aspects of the buyers' market using dark wood and bright soft furnishings which were the order of the day, in line with the trends of the mid to late '70s. But still gaslights were fitted and would be until around 1983, with some owners still being on older parks that didn't have mains supplies.

With the upturn, new makers would appear as the static holiday market strengthened; some would last months, others a few years. Some of the makers to appear from 1974 onwards were Boston, Consol, Break-away, Monarch, Didcot, Rainbow, Holidaymaker, Sunway, Country Homes, Redibuild, Atlanta, Summit, Dolphin, Sunseeker, Albion, Galaxy, Apex, Ambrose, ABC, Hudson, Volksmobil, Atlas, Zephyr, Nomad, Mercury, Ascot, Fiesta, Dalliston/Avalon, Vardo, Gold Seal, Buffalo, Fiesta, Aquilla, North Bank, Cossack, Ardax, Lissett, Kenkast and European.

Most of these new concerns were once again in the Hull area – I could fill this book just with the Hull manufacturers. But over the years the Northamptonshire area had spawned new makers joining established ones. Of these, Nene Valley was sold to the Bendix group, which also owned Cavalier touring caravans. By late 1975, Nene Valley, once a big name, would finish after twenty-five years, going into liquidation.

Nene Valley manager Roy Cattell moved to Sunseeker, whose parent company was Greens Of Brandon, and contributed greatly to their success with holiday statics and mobile homes. Similarly, Derek Upfield, formerly of Ace Caravans, began Riviera Caravans in 1969. He began manufacturing holiday statics at its Riverside works in Beverley by 1970. In 1973 the company caught up with the 'chalet holiday homes' trend,

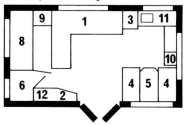

Chalet

6 Berth 18′x9′6″

P.V.C. exterior has been introduced in our new 18 foot Chalet which is fireproof, rotproof, weatherproof and is maintenance free. Double doors have again been used so that a veranda could be fitted. The lounge and dinette are an open plan design making the inside seem larger than the outside with plenty of cupboard and drawer space in the large kitchen.

The Riviera interior was designed for family accommodation with a large kitchen including an oven.

produced the Chalet, a 5.48m-long unit insulated with tin foil in the sides. For an extra cost fibreglass could be added in manufacture. Aimed at the hire fleets this holiday static had a bunk room and quite spacious lounge and rear kitchen; it had a toilet room too. Built using PVC exterior clad sides, it didn't sell. Upfield sold to Cosalt in 73/4 but he kept the factory. Riviera statics moved to a new factory and would become a whole new division of Cosalt PLC.

The 1973 Riviera Chalet was designed for letting. It had PVC-coated steel cladding and was claimed rot- and fireproof. It was dropped for 1974.

Tudor Cottage **Holiday Home**

Nene Valley Single Unit

Back in 1976 the Nene Valley Tudor Cottage was designed as a holiday home but not surprisingly with little success.

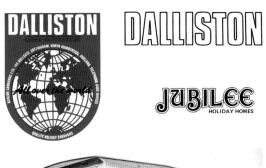

Dalliston/Avalon from 1977. Most were exported hence the exterior/interior design; they were one of many small makes around Hull.

Astral 26 shut in 1980, in its twenty-first year – this is the 26 model, one of the last to be built.

Apollo caravans was established by George Rose (ex-Lissett) and Gordon Blakeston (ex-Silverline), and built for static holiday caravans export. After the factory fire in 1975 they moved to Carnaby industrial estate, where a new factory was established. It was here too that Carnaby Caravans was established in late 1979, followed by Zephyr, which would be made at the old Riviera works, with Upfield becoming its director. By the early '80s Carnaby had begun to establish itself with popular ranges such as the value for money Crown and up market Ranchero and Ranchero Grande. Today Carnaby, along with Willerby and Pemberton, is one of the oldest established holiday home manufacturers in the UK.

Although there had been an influx of new manufacturers after the 1974/75 slump, big manufacturers such as Bluebird, A-Line, Humber, ABC, ABI, Cosalt and Astral had endured.

Memories

Andrew Jenkinson:

In the summer of 1974 I was all set to join Pemberton Caravans at their Dovedale Blackpool branch. Working on the production line I wanted to get into designing eventually, however I received a letter informing me I was no longer required due to a downturn - I was disappointed to say the least but that was the way the caravan industry worked with peaks and troughs!

But the end of 1979 began another downturn, and this time it was worse than the 1974 one. A flooded market and declining sales meant caravan factories were shutting. With caravan manufacture requiring a large supply chain, from chassis makers to window manufacturers, there was a knock-on effect both ways throughout British industry. High inflation and strikes saw manufacturers move to three-day weeks once again. Several of the big Hull makers were hit hard. Castle had increased its production from twenty to 100 statics a week in 1977 for a Dutch customer, who eventually owed Castle £250,000, spelling the end of the company. ABC/Humber had the same importer with a debt of £342,000. Big export deals that had failed shut down many caravan firms at this time, and cancelled export orders saw plenty of static holiday homes laid-up near docks, at Hull in particular.

Ci were in trouble and sold off Bluebird homes to BK in 1981, Bill Knott reacquiring his old company and renaming it BK-Bluebird. Ci subsequently crashed in December 1982. Astral and Dorchester both failed in 1980, Thomson in 1982, and Donnington in 1985. Others to fall included Fleetwind, Ardex, Jayge, Holidaymaker, Cossack and A-Line. Stag was taken over by Silverline in 1980, only for Silverline to fail in 1983, returning to make tourers only.

Pemberton's three factories also fell silent in August 1980. After the crash, the Wigan factory would get up and running in January 1981 as a workers' co-operative named Pemberton Woodhouse.

Redibuild at Full Sutton, York (with two Buccaneer Caravans directors; Mr Harrison/Mr Thundercliffe) chose a precarious time to try their hand with a new £5,368 luxury holiday home named the Chatsworth in 1979. It was advertised as having 'the charm

Opposite: Redibuild's attempt at cottage mobile home design with luxury fittings.

SILVERLINE, HOLIDAY HOMES IN BONDED PANEL SANDWICH CONSTRUCTION:

SUNSPORT

TOMORROW'S TECHNOLOGY – TODAY

This odd-looking static was built by Silverline in 1980 using bonded construction.

of old England' with its country cottage wooden beams, large fireplace and dark wood. It was a fashion trend that would last a few years and be used by several manufacturers; today it doesn't look great! But it didn't save Redibuild, which was also finished by late 1980.

There was a big culling going on, but the industry was resilient. One example is the rebirth of Paladin with its Sun Cottage in 1981. Paladin had been big in the early '60s supplying over 1,000 Sun Cottage mobile homes to London council for use by families waiting for homes. Making portable buildings the Paladin Company in 1967 had moved out of mobile homes.

In the 1980s Pemberton added new ranges, strengthening their position going into the early 1990s.

The lounge of a 1986 Willerby Granada, one of several top-selling Willerby ranges in the 1980s.

The Atlas Supreme. Atlases came up with interesting profiles and stood out on sites. (Courtesy of Holgates)

In the late '70s Paladin was going bust and it was a family connection that saved Paladin in late 1979. The two Holden daughters purchased the company from the liquidator and moved the factory to what was once the old Berkeley caravan works at Biggleswade. Now known as Broadwood the Paladin name was kept with the name Chiltern for the new 1981 Sun Cottage, but by 1986 the company had finished.

By the mid '80s an upturn gave the industry a boost. Silverline would come back, but only as a tourer producer selling off its large old Second World War aircraft hanger factory when the good days saw fifty-plus statics a week produced and a Queen's Award for Exports in 1978.

Memories

Andrew Jenkinson:

My dad had a new 1983 ABI Belmont Rio Vista 28 on Trees, a small caravan park near Ingleton, North Yorkshire. The whole family used it and we thought we were posh with its own shower and flushing loo. It slept four and gave us all years of pleasure for weeks and weekend breaks. My brother's kids loved it!

Part of the Jenkinson clan at Ingleton, posing by dad's Belmont Rio Vista in 1983.

Many caravan parks were upgraded with the addition of bars/restaurants in the early 1980s, such as this Holgates park. (Courtesy of Holgates)

Ironically Lissett homes would make a come back in late 1981 after five years' absence and would become well respected.

Similarly, Pemberton re-invented itself and turned its back on mass produced lower priced statics, concentrating on upmarket and quality ranges proving a big success to the company. Pemberton Woodhouse would establish the Pemberton name after it restarted in 1981, and by the 1990s the firm was back on course but Pemberton had moved to producing a more luxury product, which paid off with good quality and design. With seven ranges by 1991 they covered all price points where previously they just covered a basic range. Even some old model names such as Cresta, Moonbeam and Rancher were used.

Willerby, who had seen many makers come and go, would expand its markets. The mid 1980s saw Willerby launch its very successful Granada range and Lomond, and Jupiter. Willerby would also move to Hull from its factory at Willerby to a 90-acre-sized complex including storage.

Atlas, formerly Aztec, would also become innovative with new designs and distinctive looks. Atlas would be distinctive outside as well as inside and from 1976 sold well in the UK and Europe. With many popular models/ranges Atlas statics were seen on many parks and the popularity would grow by the mid 1980s. Their Supreme range, made from 1979–81, had an oval front end with five windows. It sold quite well and gave owners a talking point amongst other site users.

New makers such as Westbrook, Manor Park homes and Pinelog came about in the late '80s along with Normandie Holiday homes. Pinelog would have a short tie up with tourer manufacturers Mustang who produced a chalet-style unit. The '80s would be a time when 'holiday homes' would be the term to describe the static caravan, and mobile homes became 'park homes'. Parks now had proper designed and built clubhouses and swimming pools that would be built under cover while shops had proper mini-markets. Not all

The 1987 ABI Phoenix was a value-for-money holiday home.

parks would have this and many still offered quieter surroundings.

More firms would go bust but the caravan parks seemed to ride the storm especially those that offered good value with park fees.

Blue Anchor sensibly pulled out of holiday home and park home manufacturing and concentrated on expanding their park portfolio (Blue Anchor Leisure) with fourteen parks by 2019.

Park homemakers Tingdene and stately had expanded by the late '80s along with ABI Holiday Homes, which had become the biggest manufacturer in the UK. Their ranges included Rio Vista, Prestige, Tiffany, Phoenix and Dalesman while Cosalt had the Rivera range with popular ranges such as Torbay and Monaco. Other new makes included Delta and Arronbrook who would carve themselves a niche into the holiday home market in exports as well as the UK. Producing holiday homes only Arronbrook would also bespoke manufacture for customer requirements. Small park home manufacturer Wyresdale had set up in the late 1980s at its Poulton-le-Fylde unit producing small batches of its park homes until the late 2000s.

Delta Caravans formed in 1983 with just ten employees and became a big exporter of its wide range of holiday homes over the following decades. Although the name Fiesta had been used by Royale Precession Coachbuilding up to 1983 for statics, another shot with the Fiesta name occurred by late 1984. The new company launched two ranges, the Horizon and Gallant, aimed at the middle market.

From the 1970s the static caravan had gone through fashion trends, layouts and equipment. The U-shaped front lounge was still popular and the side dinettes but by the 1980s static users wanted more comfort and practical kitchens and larger bedrooms and washrooms. The last chapter in the static caravan story explains how park homes and holiday homes and lodges represent a new era of lifestyle; the 1990s onwards would see advances in parks as well as the homes themselves.

4 The 1990s to Now

The 1990s and beyond would see new challenges for both the manufacturer and park owner. There was a change in terminology; as the 1990s progressed the word caravan was used more and more rarely. From this chapter the mobile home is now a park home and the static is now a holiday home.

The industry had seen sales take a dive after the mid 1980s boom period with the early '90s not a good time for the holiday home industry. The '90s would see new manufacturers and into-the-millennium old names disappear and in some cases re-emerge. Hull remains the centre of holiday home manufacture in Europe, and so most new companies set up in that area.

Parks and park homes were also changing. Retirement sites, where only semi-retired over 45s could purchase, became popular. Holiday home parks were better planned with more facilities, as they began to open for longer and

Rather than having all the homes parked in a row, some new parks planned plots to provide more individual privacy.

park home manufacturers upped their game. More serious thought was given to residential parks and planning of new developments. Holiday home parks too were being redeveloped

Before...

After...

The Atlas Supreme with its round front lounge a big talking point back in the early '80s along with breakfast bars would the '90s see other innovations?

The 1980s onwards saw several companies offering park home refurbishments. By 2007 Prestige had become a manufacturer.

Prestige Homes' Hamble home interior. From renovator to park home manufacturer, Prestige has become well known in the industry.

offering more facilitates than before. Night lighting and proper roadways, holiday home park owners also tried to give plots individuality – rather than simply positioning homes in regimented rows – creating a more natural look. This attracted buyers who wanted a weekend retreat lifestyle.

In older residential parks that were still in good order, owners wanted to keep their '60s- or '70s-built homes. Several companies found their niches carrying out refurbishments. Installing UPVC windows, cladding, adding pitched roofs and upgrading interiors was a growing business from the late 1980s. This proved the launch pad for Prestige Homes, which remains a successful park home manufacturer today. Prestige was begun in 1991 by Silvano Geranio, and by the mid 1990s was manufacturing UPVC windows for the holiday and park home industry. The company grew and in 2007 went into full manufacturing of park homes. Soon they had built up a reputation for their well-designed, high-quality homes. Prestige would purchase Country Homes and by 2013 had taken over Homeseeker. The company had become a top lodge and park home manufacturer in its short time at its Rushden factory in Northamptonshire.

Cosalt, meanwhile, had moved into custom lodge building for parks, though it still manufactured holiday homes too. Cosalt were operating from the old Astral works and also owned several parks. Its tourer division, Abbey Caravans, wasn't doing as well and by 1992 was sold to Swift Caravans. Cosalt would become a leader in the park and holiday home and lodge industry.

Ercall, who had been producing luxury made-to-order park homes, went out of business by 1998. A new venture by Colin Purdy and John Swift to re-launch Mardon tourers (after they had finished in 1991) and Fiesta was to form a new company producing both tourers and holiday homes. However they finished just one

Lodges had become more popular from the 1980, and by the 1990s new lodge developments were opening. Pictured are Cosalt lodges.

year later in 1992 going into liquidation; this further enforced just how fickle the industry could be.

Galaxy homes were bought by Ivanhoe Leisure Group who also owned one time tourer manufacturer Trophy Caravans. Galaxy had some success into the early '90s with their Cameo in 1991 with its walnut wood, then fashionable finish and distinctive night lighting and luxury feel.

By 1992 Galaxy had gone out of business. However Tudor Holiday homes of Hull would take on the Galaxy name for a short time in the early to mid '90s. Tom Hudson, Hudson's Caravans founder from the '70s, had seen his holiday homes sell well. Model ranges like the Tudor Cobra was known amongst buyers along with other well-known ranges they did. Having Galaxy Tudor was hoping to increase its market share; by the mid '90s the Galaxy name was integrated with the Tudor name and models were known as Tudor Galaxy.

New manufacturers of holiday homes and park homes were always appearing even in

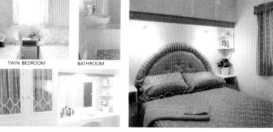

The Galaxy Cameo range was a head-turner at shows with its walnut furniture, lighting and sumptuous ambience.

Hudson took on the Galaxy name in the early '90s but never repeated the brand's success.

Fiesta built holiday homes in Hull. The image shows manufacturing and a completed Fiesta outside the factory in 1990.

a depressed market such as the mid '90s – Heritage homes, Forrester Homes, Hallmark Holiday Homes, Cambrian, Classique and Pearl Homes are justa few examples. Fiesta holiday homes ceased production by 1991. Its Legend 36 x 12 luxury home with large lounge and separate side room breakfast bar and diner had been launched for 1989. But the company faltered only to then re-appear as Hallmark Leisure Homes; the works were moved to Marfleet in Hull, the old works of defunct Sovereign/Mardon Caravans.

Meanwhile, Arronbrook homes had weathered the storm with popular models such as the Eclipse and Sunline and built up export orders as well as home market sales.

The Falcon

FALCON 28

FALCON 30

FALCON 34

FALCON 31 X 12

FALCON 35 X 12

Fiesta rolled into Hallmark Leisure Homes for 1992 but made little impact, ceasing production at the end of that year.

Arronbrook began in 1988. This is the interior of the 1992 Eclipse, showing the lounge with built-in corner sofa.

As the end of the '90s approached Atlas Homes had seen success with its Ovation and Super Ovation along with its Fanfare range and like all manufacturers was providing it in 12 wide versions. BK Bluebird would launch new model ranges but would also bring some names back from the mid '60s such as Calypso and Caprice, even the Hallmark name was used (ex-BK range) but BK Bluebird would win many design awards in the industry.

ABI, a major force in the holiday home market, became a PLC from 1990. By 1994 its products included the Rio Vista, Phoenix, Prestige and Montrose. The company's 21-acre plant was turning out holiday homes for exports too. But by the '90s this Beverley-based manufacturer was in financial trouble, struggling by 1996. Unsold tourers filled fields and heavy discounting was the writing on the wall. In the middle of 1998, ABI went into receivership. The company laid off 500 workers and a buyer was sought. ABI, once the UK's largest manufacturer of tourers, motorhomes and holiday homes, was on the brink of collapse. A lifeline was thrown and an investment company bought ABI, which was restructured and re-named ABI UK. Sections of the factory were sold off but production began with a new design team with new ideas.

By 2000 ABI UK had new ranges such as the Arizona, an entry level line-up with the Madison/Mane, York, Brisbane, Montana, and Wentworth, and a short-lived range the Victoria with pastel contemporary interior but it didn't prove popular back in 2000. Re-establishing themselves, by April 2001 ABI UK had stopped selling its tourer ranges to the nearby Swift Group. ABI would concentrate on holiday homes and within a few years a successful sales record had them back on the map and with a management buyout from the Investment Company, ABI become more innovative with new ranges and contemporary interiors.

As we entered the new millennium, the industry boomed, with parks demanding ever more holiday homes for hire and general

Atlas had launched a good number of top sellers, such as the Ovation and the Super Ovation luxury holiday homes. Note the domestic freestanding settee/chairs.

ABI UK's Victoria holiday home with its pastel interior finish. The model seems to have faltered.

The Prestige was top of the ABI range in 1994. This dark wood finish was fashionable in the '90s.

sale. In 2004 the big news was the entry into the holiday home market by tourer/ motorhome manufacturer Swift Group. The company leased a unit on Hedon Road, Hull, to design and build their first holiday homes. Swift employed George Kemp to set up production. Kemp had vast industry experience, having worked for Ace Caravans in the early 1960s and become involved with ABI holiday homes in the 1970s. The result was two ranges featuring vaulted ceilings, central lighting and contemporary interiors. Storage and good equipment was the order of the day, and with six layouts it was to be a first for Swift. By 2010 Swift had established itself as a holiday home manufacturer, going on to produce luxury lodges such as the twin Whistler.

Carnaby Holiday Homes at Bridlington had by 2002 got three ranges in their line-up, from the entry-level Chardonnay to the Champagne. Carnaby would quietly forge ahead over the years attracting a loyal following and, like most manufacturers, attending all the public shows in the UK.

For 2005 Swift moved into holiday homes, firstly with the Debut (pictured) and then the Vendee.

The interior of the Debut in 2005. Swift would quickly establish itself as a holiday home manufacturer.

Nonetheless, the landscape of manufacturers continued to shift. New manufacturers would come into play such as Oak Grove in Ireland, also Normandy, (Stellar/Corona), Heritage, Cambrian, Kingston and Europa. As the years went by new manufacturers would appear, getting a little confusing especially when companies finished only to restart again. Cosalt park homes and holiday homes were proving a hit, holiday homes especially with fleet buyers. Torbay, Rimini, Capri and Resort were just a few of the top-selling ranges.

Westbrook Holiday Homes was a Doncaster-based manufacturer that had begun in the 1980s. The company had turned heads in 1990 with the Caribbean, with its large bay window and Rattan furniture and a price tag of £16,750, but would close by 2007.

Brentmere, the Northants holiday home producer established from the ashes of Albatross Caravans, would become well known for their conventional holiday homes over the coming years being

The 2002 Carnaby Champagne boasted a vaulted ceiling, luxury seating and an opulent interior. It cost £25,665.

popular on many holiday home parks. Omar would buy the company around 1999/2000 as well as Woodbury Lodges.

In 2008 the UK hit a recession and the holiday and park home industry was hit hard. Atlas, which had around 350 workers, went out of business, as did Omar and Cosalt. Amazingly, by 2009, Atlas and Omar were back. Wonderland, established back in the 1960s, had become Wessex Homes after 1997. Wessex would be taken over in 2013 by Omar homes.

Peter Nevitt, who had been involved with Cosalt, was approached following the company's closure by a new holiday home venture. Several months went by and Victory Leisure Homes was born. By 2010 Victory had begun to export and the homes took off again using the latest trends in decor and lighting. Victory had evolved within a decade to become a major force in the lodge and holiday home industry.

Westbrook launching their distinctive bay windowed Caribbean for 1990 at a show at the G-Mex, Manchester.

Brentmere homes were distinctive and offered quality. This is the Sereno three-bed with pitched roof and brown window surrounds. Omar would buy the company by the end of the 1990s.

Cosalt were big sellers in park & holiday homes. This is the Resort, dating from 2006.

Atlas Homes had expanded over the years and its ranges were always well-received with good bedrooms and lounge-kitchens. The home pictured is from the 2004 Oasis entry-level range.

Wessex's 2018 Summer House lodge shows how modern design is influenced by the latest fashionable trends.

Sovereign, a small Coventry company building exhibition units from 1994, had by 2014 moved into park homes and lodges and in a very short time had a strong presence in the market. By 2018 they had purchased Cambrian Homes in North Wales, re-branding as Cambrian-Sovereign. Ex-management of Cambrian subsequently set up Aspire, using the old Cambrian factory at Porthmadog.

For the stalwarts, the early 2000s were a time of innovation; modernisation was the name of the game. Stately Albion and Tingdene park home manufacturers, now long established in park homes, had expanded their businesses as the park home market took off in the 2000s. Tingdene has acquired twenty parks to date; over the years it has garnered a reputation for offering park home buyers homes at the right price.

In 1992 Delta signed up with new export distributors in the Benelux countries. Within a few years investment saw state-of-the-art machinery being purchased.

By 2009 a deal was struck to supply Recreahome in Holland for their hire fleets on parks, and to also develop more parks in Holland with Delta homes which by 2010 included twin units. Now with nearly 9-acre premises and over 150 employees Delta mainly supplies export markets, though they are also sold in the UK.

Classique homes produced six ranges including in 2006 the Lodge – a 30m x 12m three-bedroom eight-berth developed for the hire fleet market, as demanded by parks that had an ever-increasing family presence.

Pemberton were now Pemberton Leisure Homes and they designed and built their Sovereign range from 1998 for disabled users. Other manufacturers such as Willerby would follow too.

Willerby had moved to a larger factory on Heddon Road (once Imperial typewriters factory) by 1989 which was further expanded and added to in the 1990s while staff increased to 400 from 250! Willerby were now the biggest holiday home producer in Europe.

Victory came out of the ashes after Cosalt pulled the plug on holiday home manufacture after 32 years; this image shows a Victory being given a check over in the factory.

Stately Albion is one of the largest park home manufacturers with an impressive selection of homes available.

The 2006 Classique Homes Lodge. It slept up to eight, so was ideal for park fleet hirers.

Delta have built up a strong European customer base. The 2001 Nordstar cost up to £12,612 for the three-bed layout.

BK Bluebird was one of the longest-running manufacturers of holiday homes. The company cleverly embraced its roots yet kept up to date, by naming its new models after old Bluebird models. One of these was the Senator, launched in 2002, with its front lounge and centrally placed gas fire. The Bluebird name would be purchased by Willerby in 2006, and Bluebird production moved to the Willerby factory. The end of holiday home manufacture in the Poole area after nearly sixty years seemed inevitable. Then a new manufacturer set up in the area named Regal Homes, maintaining the tradition of holiday home manufacture in Dorset.

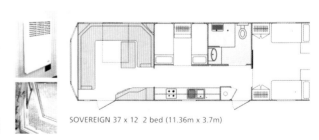

SOVEREIGN 37 x 12 2 bed (11.36m x 3.7m)

Pemberton produced its Sovereign home, designed around disabled owners, from 1998.

Willerby Homes' Hedon Road plant in the mid 1990s. By the 2000s it covered 90 acres.

The Bluebird Senator was new for 2002. A few years later Willerby purchased Bluebird and would shut the Parkstone plant down.

Regal launched after the BK/Bluebird move to Hull are based at Wareham, Dorset; this is the Regal Artisan interior kitchen/dining area.

Memories

Mike Parker:

My last holiday home was a Willerby Granada in 2005, I had it on an old established site near Blackpool. I travelled from Manchester to Blackpool after shutting the shop on Saturday evening and would return home on Sunday night. It was my escape and I could relax after a busy week. Most of my family have had holiday homes so I guess it's in our blood!

Regal would quickly expand with its contemporary interior and exterior designs.

Willerby Homes have been constantly developing new ranges and covering the market with every price point and specification. New ideas in construction and also a move into park homes as a separate division has made this company a major force abroad as well as here in the UK. With the Granada series relaunched in 2017, its range of lodges and holiday homes is staggering with every taste catered for, from the traditional to the outside-of-the-box.

Other new manufacturers have sprung up in the last few years. Some, such as Retreat Lodges, have carved themselves a niche with their architectural designs. New ideas and ways to capture a new market have been explored by many manufacturers such as ABI with their funky Rockstar lodge.

The ABI Rockstar caused a sensation at the NEC in 2018 with its funky interior.

Modern holiday homes and lodges have been getting more luxurious but now designed interiors with modern overtones (some with retro throwback too!) have given these holiday homes more appeal than ever before. Several manufacturers have also realised from customer feedback that many users have dogs and have set about adapting models to be more dog friendly such as including areas for doggy items!

Now as the story comes to an end the lodges and homes are truly superb in facilities, overall use of space and the materials used in their construction. Park homes too have again become sophisticated compared to the units of over forty years ago, and more bespoke firms have set up as customers' demands have risen. Gone are those days of long grass and poor plots; many modern holiday homes and lodges have verandas and are finished to the highest standards.

Over eighty years the concept of the holiday home and lodge have changed beyond recognition in some ways, though

Willerby launched their dog-friendly package – a feature that has proved popular, ideal for hire fleet owners who have in the past refused dogs in their fleet homes.

the basic idea of a seaside retreat or country 'cottage' still holds true today. Residential parks are better planned, with roads and high standards of living placed in some superb settings in the UK. Holiday parks have more facilities and many being owned by large groups offering families plenty to do while in a holiday home. There have been many manufacturers over the years and more to follow no doubt. The new leisure homes of 2019 are light years away from those ideas tried over the years but all new models owe much to the heritage of the static caravan that has become Britain's favourite holiday home!

The interior of the 2018 Atlas Trend has retro-contemporary styling.

The modern park home is a popular choice for retirement, as this 2019 Willerby Delamere 50x22 twin unit demonstrates, with its contemporary decor, good use of space, high finish and specification.

Residential parks offer better plots and full services with good road systems in place – a far cry from a caravan stuck in a field!

Modern holiday homes have domestic fitted kitchens, as seen in this Arronbrook Eclipse.

Opposite and above: A Pathfinder 10 wide, still in use in 2017 at Pathfinder Village Park, and a 2018 Pathfinder at the Lawns trade show. Fifty-seven years separates these two models. What will the next fifty-plus years see in park and holiday home design?